T0034966

THE BLESSED LIFE

THE BLESSED LIFE

A 90-DAY DEVOTIONAL
THROUGH THE TEACHINGS
AND MIRACLES OF JESUS

KELLY MINTER

Printed in China

978-1-0877-6691-1

Published by B&H Publishing Group
Brentwood, Tennessee

Dewey Decimal Classification: 226.93
Subject Heading: BIBLE. N.T. MATTHEW 5–9 / CHRISTIAN LIFE / DEVOTIONAL LITERATURE

Cover design by Faceout Studio, Lindy Kasler. Cover images by Javier Pardina/Stocksy; mxbfilms/Shutterstock; 8H/Shutterstock; robert_s/Shutterstock. Author photo by Micah Kandros.

1 2 3 4 5 6 • 26 25 24 23

To my parents and all the wonderful believers at Reston Bible Church who taught me the ways of the Blessed Life by teaching me Jesus.

ACKNOWLEDGMENTS

WRITING A BOOK IS A solo endeavor and yet somehow the end product is a group effort of inestimable proportions. I have many dear companions who accompanied me on this journey through Jesus's teachings and healings: Dallas Willard, John Stott, Jonathan Pennington, Dietrich Bonhoeffer, Scot McKnight, Craig Blomberg, and Stanley Hauerwas were my closest confidents throughout, though I've never personally met any of them. What a gift their humble spirits and years of scholarship have been to me.

I am immensely thankful to my publisher and editor Ashley Gorman, a champion of this project from the beginning, as well as an academic, wordsmith, and theologian. Her expertise and keen eye brought so much to this devotional. My agent Lisa Jackson, too, is a wise listener and cultivator of ideas who supported me on this journey. I am forever indebted to Lifeway and B&H for their reach and support of me over nearly two decades—especially to those on this project like Kim Stanford, Jade Novak, Susan Browne, and Whitney Alexander who turn ideas on a screen into beautiful realities. It's a wonderful treasure when publishers become friends.

I'm indebted to Rolling Hills Community Church and Justice & Mercy International for being the communities of life-long friends you are. I'm also deeply thankful for the professors at Denver Seminary who have stretched my heart and mind further than I thought they could go.

Above all, I wholeheartedly acknowledge my family—Mom, Dad, Megan, Katie, David, Brad, Megen, Maryn, Emmett, Holland, Will, Harper and Lily; and my dear friends—April, Mary Katharine, and Paige who take black and white words on a page and give them color and meaning. For me, you are what make *The Blessed Life* blessed indeed. All because of Jesus. I would have nothing without Him.

CONTENTS

INTRODUCTION

This devotional is for anyone who wants to take a fresh look at the person of Jesus. To listen anew to what He says and behold once again His healing touch and unspeakable power. Our world has a lot to say about Jesus, but what if we sat down on an ancient Galilean hillside together and listened to Him speak for Himself? What if we then followed Him down the mountain and watched Him reach out to outsiders and outcasts, wanderers and worriers with astounding care and compassion?

I imagine it would change our lives.

I want to warmly welcome you to this ninety-day journey through the teachings and miracles of Jesus. Day by day and verse by verse, we'll stroll through Jesus's Sermon on the Mount and ten of His most notable miracles. We will gain the most practical insights into our relationships, our possessions, our purpose, and the way God intends for us to live most freely and abundantly. I'll do my best to shed light on the cultural context, occasionally highlight the original language, and make logical connections where they're not always obvious. Mostly, I will try to get at the heart of what Jesus is saying and doing so we can find clarity for our paths and healing for our souls. So we can be His actual disciples in a world desperate for earnest Christ-followers.

I also want to note that whether you are a seasoned believer, new to the Christian faith, or simply exploring Jesus, I am expectant this book will meet you where you're at. And if you have ever found Jesus's teachings to be confusing, heavy, or out of touch, my prayer is that a fresh listen and look will be healing and rejuvenating for your soul. Also, if you've known Jesus's commands but have lost sight of His love, I can't wait to follow Him with you straight to the sick, marginalized, religious and non-religious alike. The matchless power and love He brought to bear upon those He encountered is still at work in our lives today.

I must admit that up until the past several years, the Sermon felt like an unrelated string of nearly impossible teachings I couldn't always make sense of. If I could oversimplify my problem, it was this: I had looked to Jesus as my Savior (His death and resurrection) and to the New Testament epistles for how to live the Christian life. This meant I'd not spent much time studying what Jesus said about being salt and light in our broken world, what it means for our actions and our hearts to align, how to live generously, unhindered by worry and anxiety, which acts of goodness to show and which ones to keep private, how to pray, how to prioritize, how to build a life on solid ground. In other words, how to live *The Blessed Life*. And I certainly had not made the connection between all that Jesus taught and His immediate plunge into a sea of hurting people—like you and me—who desperately needed His healing touch, His compassion, and most of all, His *Godness*.

It was the Gospel writer Matthew who first paired Jesus's famous teaching (Matt. 5–7) with ten handpicked miracles (Matthew 8–9), and it made sense to follow his lead in this devotional. I imagine he did this so we might know that Jesus is not only a fountain of wisdom but also an ocean of love—what He taught He lived, and He wants the same for us.

So if I could distill my hope for you over the next 90 days it is this: that every day you'll learn more about how to live the life Jesus says is *blessed* and be overwhelmed by His immeasurable power and tenderness. My heart is eager for you, new and dear friend. What a well of wisdom and compassion Jesus is for those who will come to Him. What purpose there is for your life, what hope, what joy, what reconciliation and renewal await. If only you will simply follow Him.

PART 1
THE TEACHINGS OF JESUS

Part 1 of this devotional covers Jesus's most extensive collection of teachings found in Matthew chapters 5–7, best known to us as The Sermon on the Mount. I encourage you to prepare your heart for what Jesus has to say to you over the next sixty days. Perhaps keep a journal close by, noting what stands out and what you can implement in your everyday life. Jesus's words were meant to be imparted and lived.

So I invite you to find a comfortable spot on that Galilean hillside where we will simply listen to what Jesus has to say and then seek to obey Him. When we stand back up at the end of His hope-filled message, my prayer is that we'll follow Him down the mountain with more understanding, purpose, and love than we had when we first sat down.

DAY 1

MATTHEW'S PURPOSEFUL PEN

"Now Jesus began to go all over Galilee, teaching in their synagogues, preaching the good news of the kingdom, and healing every disease and sickness among the people."

Matthew 4:23

"Jesus continued going around to all the towns and villages, teaching in their synagogues, preaching the good news of the kingdom, and healing every disease and every sickness."

Matthew 9:35

If someone asked you to describe Jesus's ministry on earth in a single sentence, what words would you use to describe it? We begin our ninety-day journey together with a single sentence from the book of Matthew answering this question. I suppose it's actually two sentences, but it's the same one stated twice: Jesus *taught* in the synagogues, *preached* the good news of the kingdom, and *healed* many people in the towns and villages in and around Galilee. Matthew wants us to know lots of things about Jesus's ministry, but he really wants us to know *these* three things. How do we know this? Because verses 4:23 and 9:35 serve as repetitive bookends that each *declare* what Jesus did on either side of Matthew *showing* us what He did (scholars call this literary device an *inclusion*).

This doubly stated sentence is the heartbeat of our devotional. It's the summary of the primary elements of Jesus's mission, but we will soon find that Matthew never intended for us to settle for a summary. He wants us to immerse ourselves in the details. To sit on the verdant hillside listening to Jesus's wisdom, to be bowled over by the astonishing good news of His kingdom, to follow Him through a sea of hurting people for whom He had come to touch and heal. Matthew wants us to *experience* Jesus.

Are you languishing? Is your hope waning? Perhaps your mind is unsettled, or your body is fighting disease, or you're emotionally spent because of deep loss or ongoing pain. Or you might simply need some direction, a bit of guidance. Or maybe you're just desperate for an encounter with Him.

No matter why you're here, you're in the right place, for we can't linger in the presence of Jesus and not be changed. Not be renewed.

So let us step into first-century Galilee, a region in the northern countryside of Judea. Let's brush up against the Jewish people who were plodding along under Roman occupation, mostly as struggling farmers, fishermen, or subsistence laborers.[1] A population that by modern standards lived in poverty, some of whom were considered outcasts and expendables.[2] Let's nestle beside them in the grassy field and listen to Jesus because He first announces His kingdom to precisely *this* group.

This, all by itself, is cause for us to lean in.

The Son of God. The incarnate One. The "late in time" Messiah for whom Israel had long been waiting had finally come! It would stand to strategic reason, even basic common sense, that Jesus would leak the breaking news of His kingdom in the Jerusalem courts of the religious elite. Or perhaps He might seek an audience with the wealthy minority or the Roman emperors. His best bet by a mile would be to approach any number of these powerful waterheads of the fastest moving streams where big news travels fast.

But Jesus is no politician. His kingdom is not of this world.

How unconventional for Jesus to deliver His otherworldly ethic—the truths about how we're to live and who we can now be as new people—on the side of a hill to a noninfluential gathering of the downtrodden. When we'd expect Him to go where the power is, He goes to where the need is. Here we discover that the good news of Jesus Christ will not go from the top down but from the bottom up, or perhaps I should say bottom *out*, to the ends of the earth.

What hope-filled days we have ahead, and what a gift Matthew has given us! A curated collection of Jesus's words and deeds; a peek into the struggles of His primary followers; a detailed record of what He deemed most important about how we're to live the precious lives we've been given; a collection of specific people He cleansed, touched, healed, challenged, called, and poured compassion on. In all these ways and more, Matthew has clearly not left us haphazard memories from his morning journal; rather his pen is purposeful and passionate.

What is your need? What are your longings? Carry them into the presence of Jesus and hear what He has to say. He has much to tell and show us over the next ninety days.

And if you feel undeserving, or unspectacular, or ordinary . . .

If you identify as burdened . . .

The anxious.

The bottom dweller.

The non-pious believer . . .

Do not despair. He has come for you.

DAY 2

THE PEOPLE ON THE HILLSIDE

"Then the news about him spread throughout Syria. So they brought to him all those who were afflicted, those suffering from various diseases and intense pains, the demon-possessed, the epileptics, and the paralytics. And he healed them. Large crowds followed him from Galilee, the Decapolis, Jerusalem, Judea, and beyond the Jordan."

Matthew 4:24–25

While a few of Jesus's earliest disciples appear to be His primary audience, and we will get to them soon, we must not forget the others who populated the hillside that day—those craning their ears over the disciples' shoulders. Today's passage tells us just what type of people generally made up the crowds who followed Jesus. As we touched on yesterday, they were the hurting, those on the fringes of society, the diseased, paralyzed, pain stricken. The demon possessed.

We must get out of our heads images of crisp, gingham picnic blankets spread about with well-kempt middle-class families sitting in linen sundresses and ironed button-ups, snacking on baguettes and cheese while listening to Jesus give a Sunday school lesson. Those to whom Jesus first announced His kingdom were a desperate, mostly impoverished, hardscrabble lot. We aren't given details about how controlled the setting was on the day Jesus delivered His Sermon, but I imagine it was a somewhat rambunctious scene of restless children, hungry babies fussing, and the sick moaning. Perhaps some were asking questions or dissenting.

When I imagine that day's setting, I think back to one of my first trips to the Amazon jungle with Justice & Mercy International (JMI). We were in a village partnering with an indigenous pastor to assist with a day camp and worship service for kids and families among the *riberinhos* (people of the river). It was a sweltering day where the humidity wrapped itself around me like extended relatives on Christmas, and there wasn't an air-conditioned building within a thousand miles. From our boat we unloaded guitars and a djembe for worship; crayons, construction paper, and glue for crafts; and reams of pasta for lunch.

My vision of an orderly service where information would be transmitted from one party to the other with an end result of people's lives being on-the-spot transformed by Christ was about to be tweaked (read: dashed). What instead transpired was a chaos I wasn't used to in our orderly American church services where squirming babies are slipped into special rooms with rocking chairs and the distracted feign attention. Moms pressed forward for prayer, sporadically calling out for the needs of their families. Kids poked and prodded one another. Toddlers walked up to their mother's breasts and started nursing—standing up. The men swatted away flies with one hand and swiped sweat from their brows with the other. Everyone was eager for the meal we'd prepared to serve after the service. Few seemed to be paying attention to the worship songs I'd taken the time to learn in Portuguese—the nerve.

If the goal was orderly conduct and listeners' absorbing information I deemed important, it was an utterly disastrous worship service. But when I consider that Jesus met physical and emotional needs, in addition to spiritual ones, that day proved a turning point for me. In hindsight, it was a classic case of my having no concept of what it's like to wake up in the morning and spear fish, feed mouths who may or may not be your own offspring, lumber to the closest outlet for clean water, tend your family's diseases with your own bare hands—all while praying to God your husband comes home with a hunted animal that can be carved into stew for dinner. I needed to be reminded that Jesus cares for the whole person.

The physical needs of the *riberinhos* in many ways resemble the ones of Jesus's first-century followers. As they listened to His famous Sermon on that patch of earth, they did so not as those without need but as those deeply in touch with their need. How remarkable and tender that Jesus didn't only address their spiritual depravation without also being keenly sensitive to address physical and emotional needs too. (Matthew's intentional pairing of His teachings and healings affirms this reality.) And how important is the reminder to you and me that whatever the specific scene looked like on that hillside, we can know for sure the ordinary and the suffering believed Jesus had a place for them.

This is good news for those who have assumed they can only approach God in their Sunday best. It's good news for the ones who have tried everyone and everything else only to be disappointed. And it's good news for those who feel on the outside because if this passage tells us anything, it says, *you belong.*

So before you sit down in the tall grass to listen to Jesus, the Teacher, may you first take in this good news. May you receive the reminder that He is not one to pass over your needs, pain, longings, loneliness. . . . He is not simply about transferring information but transferring a kingdom to you. Yes, He has truths upon which you can build your house, ethics that will shape your decision making, wisdom that will confound your instincts. But you will only revel in Him as Teacher because He has first given Himself to you as Savior.

What needs do you need Him to address today? He invites you to bring them.

DAY 3

WHAT IS THE KINGDOM OF HEAVEN?

"Now Jesus began to go all over Galilee . . . preaching the good news of the kingdom."

Matthew 4:23

As anxious as I am to get to the Sermon on the Mount, we still have a bit of groundwork to lay. I'd hate for us to jump into scene 1 without a good handle on some key themes. (It would be like touring the White House after having snoozed through American history class; you'd appreciate the décor and savor the honor, but you'd miss the stories hidden in the paintings and architecture.) So we must begin by looking at this idea of the ***kingdom of heaven***. It is a central topic of Jesus's teaching and ministry. Matthew uses the phrase fifty-five times in his Gospel alone, and it's one of the first phrases Jesus mentions in His Sermon on the Mount.[3] And since the kingdom of heaven is hopelessly intertwined with human flourishing, we really do want to understand it.[4]

Trying to succinctly define the kingdom of heaven is like attempting to define wind or your favorite novel. One of my favorite seminary professors describes it as "the in-breaking of God into history to realize his redemptive purposes," and I find this helpful.[5] He goes on to explain that Christ's kingdom "is a reign more than a realm, a power rather than a place."[6] If I can attempt to put it into my own words, I would say it's anything having to do with Christ's being, character, or actions made manifest in our broken world, primarily through His people, by the power of the Holy Spirit, as a result of Christ's coming to earth. I shall receive no extra points for brevity or precision.

To use the old adage, the kingdom is a concept better caught than taught. This must surely be why Jesus spoke of it in parables when trying to explain its nature. It's like a mustard seed, He said, yeast working its way through dough, a hidden treasure, a merchant seeking a priceless pearl, a fisherman's net!

For all its complexities, it's good to be reminded that one way Jesus described the kingdom is simply that it is *good news.*

In what area of your life do you yearn for the kingdom of heaven to come? Where do you want the in-breaking of His goodness, peace, and "rightness" to touch down in your life? Where are you desperate for His presence? We will have lots of time to further consider what exactly it is. Right now I want you to think about where you want it to come.

Which brings us to another important aspect of the kingdom of heaven—it is *at hand* (Matt. 4:17). It is within our grasp, close enough to touch, accessible enough to enter (Matt. 7:13, 21). We must leave behind our notions of slogging it out on earth in our own strength until we get to some way faraway place called heaven when we die (though resurrection and heaven on earth are surely coming for us one day). We have the power and the goodness and the beauty and the righteousness of God's kingdom available to us *now* because the presence of the King is among us.

What specifically does this look like, you may wonder. We will spend the next eighty-seven days exploring the answer to this question. In the meantime, it looks like having the power to love those who have wronged you, possess joy through adversity, cast off anxiety when there's lots to worry about, commune intimately with God when sin used to be a barrier. It is a brand-new way of living in the power of the Spirit, wholly counter to the empty promises of the world in which we live. In a word, it means to live the life Jesus called *blessed.*

The secret to living in this glorious kingdom, you ask. The arrival of the King.

Dearest Jesus, give us a vision of Your kingdom as we study your wise teachings and compassionate actions. Show us what it means to live the blessed life according to Your Word and how it can change our lives now.

DAY 4

JESUS, THE TEACHER

"When he saw the crowds, he went up on the mountain, and after he sat down, his disciples came to him. Then he began to teach them."

Matthew 5:1–2

I HAVE A SPECIAL PLACE in my heart for teachers. They pass on to us knowledge about the world and ourselves that we otherwise wouldn't know. They help us hone skills and master tools that allow us to navigate our lives. They believe in us. Teachers have shown me where to place my fingers on the fret board of a guitar and how to strum in time. In high school, coaches drilled into me the optimal form of shooting a basketball. *Use your wrist. Don't forget to put your legs into your shot. Follow through.* My seminary professors have waltzed me through the maze of church history, Israel's monarchy, the Gospels, and took the lead through tricky books like Ezekiel.

I will never get over that of all the things Jesus could have done for a hurting, dejected, oppressed crowd, He chose to *teach* them. This is not an obvious move when you take into account the makeup of the listeners and their needs (Matt. 4:24). This would have been a fine time for multiplying some loaves and fish. A healing service would have really hit the nail on the head.

But Jesus taught . . .

Of course He tended to physical and emotional needs too, but He determined that at the inauguration of His kingdom on earth, one of the most meaningful treasures He could entrust to His disciples and share with the listening crowds was truth. Wisdom. Knowledge. And not only knowledge about how the world works and how the people in the world tend to tick, but even more compelling, how life works in His kingdom and how the people of His kingdom are now empowered to live with new and soft hearts filled with His Spirit. His big reveal on that mountainside, then, was not *how you can have entirely different circumstances in five easy steps,* but rather, *how you can be an entirely new person in the face of any circumstance.* We in the kingdom of God can walk through this world differently, namely because Jesus walks with us.

Are you fuzzy as to the purpose of your life? Are you wondering if trials and loneliness mean God has forsaken you? Have years of trying to get even with your ex-boyfriend or ex-boss or ex-best friend left you exhausted and bitter? Has anxiety wound itself around you like a sea nettle because you're not sure how college will get paid for, or if your wayward child will return, or if the disease is back? Do you pursue God to puff up your ego as people applaud your religious deeds, or have you learned the secret of your prayer closet? Have you constructed your life's house on sand that gives way the moment the winds roll onto shore, or on immovable, unshakable rock?

Jesus will address this and so much more in His Sermon on the Mount. And this is not used-car salesman speak. With economy of words and power of speech, Jesus will teach us how to live well as defined by our heavenly Father. He will pull forth from His storehouse treasures old and new (Matt. 13:52) that will thrill and amaze.

But, first, one thing. We must hold loosely what we think we know. As we learn from Jesus, it will help to take the posture of a child learning from his mother how to tie his shoe, or from a father how to bait her hook. We must assume that some of what feels innate to us will, surprisingly enough, work against us as we discover the counterintuitive culture of the kingdom of heaven. And some of what would typically seem like death will actually produce life. What we can know for sure is that if we will learn from Him, and obey accordingly, we will be *blessed.* After all, this is the first word of His beloved teaching.

Lord, prepare my heart for what's ahead. Make me ready for what you have to say and then help me live out your good and life-giving words.

DAY 5

WHAT IT MEANS TO BE BLESSED

"Blessed are the poor in spirit, for the kingdom of heaven is theirs."

Matthew 5:3

Sometimes when I'm really out of sorts, my friends will remind me of how truly blessed I am, how much I have to be thankful for. But this always feels like an evasion to me, like they're not giving my "pain and suffering" its due. They're looking for what *is* going well in my life, doing the math, and then deciding I've got more going for me in the *blessed* column than in the *poor in spirit* one, so blessed it is.

I don't know how the word *blessed* hit Jesus's disciples on the hillside that day or how it landed on the crowds, but I can't imagine it was the first word the sick, lame, shunned, or hungry expected to hear Him speak to them that day. And Jesus wasn't using the word to convince them that the good things in their life outweighed the bad, that they were more blessed than not. He was declaring those in His kingdom as wholesale flourishing.

Blessed.

Think of that word hanging out there over a Jewish people hobbling under Roman oppression. The ones who for centuries had been pining for a powerful Messiah in the image of King David to knock their enemies out of the land. Surely some had followed Jesus out of curiosity but most out of pure desperation. Some were longing for a new leader who could help them figure out how to get back on the God of Israel's good side, someone with a solid campaign slogan. Some may have showed up hoping to hear a strategic and gutsy military plan: *Who's ready to defeat Rome once and for all? Strap on your swords!* Others may have been looking for something more personal and close to home, like a much needed healing or handout.

Blessed.

The word itself is not an unusual opener. It's only shocking when you think about whom He addressed it to: the poor in spirit, mourners, stomped on, hungry, innocent, persecuted. Well, now, this just feels like madness. How can the poor in spirit be the blessed ones? In what kind of a world, in what kind of a kingdom, in what kind of a religion, has this ever been so?

Before we consider an answer, it is worth asking, Why are *you* here? Why have you come to listen to the words of Jesus?

Are you looking for Him to overpower someone who has wounded you? Is a family member sick and in need of healing? Are finances tight? Is work unfulfilling? Is your marriage suffering? Are you simply tired of the grind, like the average Jewish peasant in first-century Galilee looking for a sustaining word of encouragement, a change in the political landscape? Perhaps you're not looking for anything from Him as much as you simply want to be with Him and listen to what He has to say.

Note that the "them" Jesus begins to teach in verse 2 appear to be His disciples. But at the end of His message, it was the crowds who were astonished at His teaching (Matt. 7:28). We should establish at the outset that both disciples and undecideds are invited to listen. Whichever you are, I'm glad you're here.

But back to our question. How can people like the poor in spirit be blessed? In the original language, the word for "blessed" is *makarios*, and it means "prospering, fortunate, flourishing," and in some cases, "downright happy." (This is different from the word used when someone pronounces a blessing on another, translated *eulogeo*). *Makarios* is a description of *the state* of a person who is thriving in the kingdom of God. So Jesus isn't saying that the poor in spirit will eventually gain a blessing. He is saying that their current state of being is a prosperous one because God's kingdom is *theirs*. In fact, in every case of the nine Beatitudes, a difficult state of being is paired with a promise of blessing.

So if you're struggling or hurting today, may Jesus redefine your circumstances as only He can. If you find yourself poor in spirit, malnourished by the "blessings" of our culture, you're in prime position to experience the blessed life of the kingdom.

Ask Him to teach you and show you what it means to flourish in whatever your circumstances. Look for Him to answer you as you go about Your day. He is eager to meet you in it.

DAY 6

THE BLESS-EDS

"Blessed are the poor in spirit . . . those who mourn . . . the humble . . . those who hunger and thirst for righteousness . . . the merciful . . . the pure in heart . . . the peacemakers . . . [the] persecuted."

Matthew 5:3–10

As a child who grew up in Sunday school, I was familiar with the Beatitudes, but I must admit they never really drew me in. They felt like an arduous list of to-dos, but even worse, who wanted to try to be poor in spirit, or hungry, or, for heaven's sake, persecuted? In high school I found this less enticing than being popular. While a great deal of sanctification still needed to happen in my life, at least some of my aversion to the Beatitudes was simply that I didn't understand them.

Without stripping the Beatitudes of their radical claims, it came as a great relief to learn that the Beatitudes are not a list of Christian to-dos. Nor are they Paul's fruit of the Spirit we're to display, or the Ten Commandments we're to carefully adhere to. They are antigravity truths that float up when the harshness of life crashes down. They are more like laws of nature than laws of the land. You don't keep the Beatitudes like a good citizen; rather you live by them as fundamentally sound realities you can count on.

Jonathan Pennington explains them this way, "Jesus presents not a list of heroes of the faith nor a list of moral behaviors that describe the truly pious but rather a redefinition of who the people of God are."[7] Don't you just love this?

This liberates me, and I hope it does you too. The Beatitudes are not another diet plan or exercise regime or study program on which you need to get cracking. They're a declaration of how life operates in God's kingdom since the arrival of Jesus! They're promises of what's available to us right now and in the age to come.

If we're really going to "get" the Beatitudes, I think the most helpful thing to do is put ourselves in the shoes of who was there that day. We must stand on the hillside of the worn out, those weary of waiting for God to bring freedom from their oppressors like He promised Abraham He would. Maybe you are already in those shoes—poor in spirit, mournful, having to show mercy . . . again. You've had it up to here with sticking yourself in between two warring parties as the peacemaker. Being pure in heart has cost you your place in line. Belonging to the pious doesn't seem worth it.

It is precisely in these conditions that Jesus speaks the word *blessed*. He says *you* are flourishing in His kingdom because of divine realities His presence calls into existence.

If we listen to the Beatitudes, as those first-century followers of Jesus listened, I believe they will ring out as kingdom realities, not kingdom chores. If you're mourning, you're invited to flourish in God's kingdom because you can count on being comforted by the Son of God Himself. If someone has deeply wronged you, you're invited to be merciful to the wrongdoer because Christ will, without a doubt, shower you with His mercy. If you find yourself persecuted for the sake of Christ, you can reckon yourself as positively blessed because the kingdom of heaven is *yours*. This is still as radical as ever; it's just no longer oppressive.

As we consider the Beatitudes over the next nine days, don't feel like you have to *do* anything. Jesus has plenty for us to do later in the Sermon. For now, cease striving and simply contemplate the surprising nature of Christ's kingdom. Reflect on the deep mystery of being able to thrive in the presence of Christ when the world says *impossible*. And if you struggle to understand what some of the Beatitudes mean, it's okay. Rest assured we will spend the rest of our lives growing into them. You need only make yourself available to learning His ways.

DAY 7

BLESSED ARE THE POOR IN SPIRIT

"Blessed are the poor in spirit, for the kingdom of heaven is theirs."

Matthew 5:3

This is the first of the nine *macarisms*, or blessings. In the strangest twist of events, Jesus is declaring that the insiders of His kingdom are not the Jews who have been above average in their Torah observance. They aren't necessarily the Bible study filler-outters, the choir directors, the mission trippers. Neither are they the wealthy elite who don't really need God because they've figured out how to make life work on their own terms.

No, Jesus says the poor in spirit are the insiders, those who are acutely aware of their inability to measure up, who know their need for God across the board. Interestingly, Luke's Gospel simply says "the poor" are blessed, creating a bit of dispute around what Jesus means here. But I don't think we have to choose between physical poverty and spiritual poverty. Both conditions can put us in prime position to experience the wealth of Christ's kingdom because both conditions typically lead us to the end of ourselves.

I cannot claim to have ever lived in poverty, but my first several years in Nashville were—how shall I put this?—*lean*. I was a struggling musician on every front. There was at least one month when my landlord let me live rent free, and this was not for lack of my working at several tasks outside of trying to become famous. I was a fence-staining, lawn-mowing, garage-cleaning worker for whoever would have me. My college friends were all back in Virginia crushing it in politics or banking, getting married, and building brick homes. I was on a sinking vessel otherwise known as the music industry and, by middle-class standards, "poor." I was not just financially so but equally struggling on the continuum of well-being.

During these years in particular, I discovered the reverse nature of the Beatitudes. As one clever thinker says about them, "Jesus here takes us through the sound barrier, where things begin to work backwards."[8] In other words, those in the most unblessed conditions are the ones Jesus describes as thriving because of His promise that the kingdom of heaven belongs to them. Ironically, the poor in spirit (the ones who have little of what the world values) possess the belongings the rich in spirit (the ones who seemingly have everything) can't acquire.

During this several-year stretch when I experienced this irony, I met Christ in a way I had never before known Him. If you've lived on this fallen earth long enough, you know what I mean. It's those times when we lose our job, can't pay our bills, fail at a dream, or face abandonment by a loved-one—and we don't know what to do. Being poor in spirit can also mean reaching the top of our game and discovering we're hauntingly unfulfilled. No matter how we arrive there, it often takes becoming "poor" in the world's kingdom to understand what it means to inherit the true wealth of the kingdom of heaven.

In ancient times the materially poor had only God as their refuge. The term *poor* had taken on spiritual significance.[9] Like when David said of himself, "This poor man cried, and the LORD heard him and saved him from all his troubles" (Ps. 34:6). Or more significantly, when Jesus interpreted the prophet Isaiah's hope for the poor as being about Himself, "He has anointed me to preach good news to the poor" (Luke 4:18; Isa. 61:1).

For the ancient listener, this first beatitude didn't come out of the blue. To be poor and know God's favor was certainly in keeping with Old Testament values and prophecies. The radical part was that the poor in spirit were suddenly the flourishing ones because Jesus was bestowing His kingdom to *them*. This must have felt like the other side of the sound barrier for Jesus's followers. It should feel like that for us, too.

In the strangest turn of events, it is the undeserving in need of grace for whom the King is holding open the door to His kingdom. The humble are surpassing the self-righteous and self-reliant on their way inside.

So, dear one, take heart in your struggle and hold your head high in the places where you tend to feel low. To be poor in spirit is to know the riches of God. It's to know the kingdom of heaven that is *yours* in Christ.

DAY 8

BLESSED ARE THOSE WHO MOURN

"Blessed are those who mourn, for they will be comforted."

Matthew 5:4

I WAS RUSHING TO GET home when I got caught at a railroad crossing, something I find to be excessively torturous. It's the interminable nature of it, the not knowing how many train cars there are, the regret of not having chosen a different way home. But this is also the upside of a train—that it can span a distance, that the locomotive and caboose remain attached even if separated by a mile. The Beatitudes are a bit like trains. We can think of the condition of each as the locomotive and its corresponding promise as the caboose. Whatever sequence of life or waiting or faith is in between, they're inseparably one.

We must keep the caboose (the promise) in mind, especially when considering "blessed are those who mourn," a statement so paradoxical that John Stott says it's equivalent to "happy are the unhappy."[10] This only makes sense if we keep in view its unflagging guarantee: the mourners *will be comforted.*

I wish for this beatitude to wash over you with hope today. Whatever profound loss, whatever ache refuses to be quieted, the comfort of Christ is overflowing for you now (2 Cor. 1:3–5).

For the people on the Galilean hillside, at least part of what was causing them a great deal of sadness and grief was the loss of their land. They were exiles in their own country. Remember, the Romans were in charge. Before that, Israel had lost Solomon's temple to Babylon, and things after the exile never went back to the way they'd been before. Much of their mourning had to do with the collective pain they as the covenant people of God had endured for centuries. They were mourning over that which had yet to come.

And isn't this so often what we mourn over? What we no longer have? Or what we've never had?

The Jews' own prophet Isaiah spoke of a day when a Messiah would bind up the brokenhearted, proclaim freedom for the captives, release prisoners from darkness, and, yes, *comfort those who mourn* (Isa. 61). Part of the comfort would come through ancient ruins being restored and cities long devastated being rebuilt. In other words, the promised land would once again be theirs. But the wait had been long and the grind wearying. The disciples and crowds couldn't have imagined that the One teaching them that day was the Comforter of whom Isaiah had spoken.

Perhaps you are mourning. And maybe not over something that just didn't work out the way you'd hoped but over a loss you considered firmly entrenched in God's will and ways, just as Jesus's ancient listeners were. I think of Hannah who wept over not being able to have a child, a specific blessing God bestowed on a man and woman's union (Gen. 1:28). How could God withhold from Hannah what God had ordained? What about God directing Abraham to offer up Isaac when Isaac was the child of promise? Or Joseph being "sent by God" from the promised land of Canaan into slavery, to the pagan nation of Egypt? These are inescapable ironies.[11] And yet they are not ironies through which our Savior Himself hasn't lived: "My God, my God, why have you abandoned me?" (Matt. 27:46), cried Jesus.

The best part of today's beatitude is that the One who promises to comfort you is the One who knows your grief, has carried your diseases, intimately knows rejection, and bore the title, "Man of Sorrows" (see Isa. 53:3 ESV). *That* Jesus is the One whose arms are open wide to you and longs to comfort you in your confusion and sorrow. When you choose to lament in His presence, Jesus says, this is what it means to flourish. Not as a result of your circumstances but because Christ's comfort meets you in those circumstances. And the comfort you know in part today will one day be known in full. The caboose is on its way.

DAY 9

BLESSED ARE THE MEEK

"Blessed are the meek, for they will inherit the earth."

Matthew 5:5 NIV

JESUS'S THIRD BEATITUDE CUTS STRAIGHT to our desire for control, to protect our rights, to get back at anyone who tries to take what's ours. To respond in meekness to those who threaten our possessions, property, or people goes against our every propensity because meekness has to do with self-control and peacemaking. So it's a funny thing that meekness is often associated with the rhyming word *weakness*, or as being timid or mousy, when there's hardly a more robust attribute out there.

As we settle back in beside Jesus's first-century listeners, the first question we need to ask is, What in the world does inheriting the earth have to do with meekness? For starters, it helps if *earth* is translated *land*, as in the promised land. As one commentator humorously states, "Those to whom Jesus spoke didn't care two figs for owning Italy or Gaul. They simply wanted shalom in the Land of Israel."[12] (The early church viewed Jesus's words about the earth more widely, including the entire world as being the inheritance of those with faith in Christ; see Rom. 4:13.)

And, no surprises here, there were a *lot* of opinions in Israel about how to get the land back. While the Pharisees hoped that law-keeping would coerce God into restoring to them the land, the Zealots wanted to take it by force. The temptation was to look to a charismatic political leader or a strong military to get back what had once been theirs.

I wonder what you want back, or what you're afraid might be taken away? The even more important question is, *How* do you intend to right past wrongs or protect what you have? Are you worried or vengeful? Is bitterness gnawing at your insides? Is your hope in people, power, or money, or have you set your hope fully on Jesus and what He promises to provide?

When our propensity is to fight, Jesus says this, in essence:

> *Blessed are you when you trust Me to fulfill what God has promised you. Drop your swords. Stop trying to control outcomes through religious effort. Don't adapt to the world to gain the world or run from it to overcome it. To the contrary, humbly wait on the Father to bring justice and the full arrival of His kingdom. Determine to forgo getting even and taking what may even be rightfully yours by demand or force, because I've already secured the world for you.*

A few years ago, I had my property surveyed for a fence. Just as the stakes went in to mark my plot of earth, my exceedingly crotchety neighbor at the time, the one who had lived in the house next door for more than fifty years, waltzed up my driveway carrying a stack of papers that included a plat from the days of antiquity. He said I was over his property line by at least a foot. Never mind the professionals I'd hired to determine my lot lines, the ones who came with lasers.

His lack of kindness and his "papers" unsettled me. My house and my yard, after all, is the only place on this entire globe I get to call my own. It's my miniscule version of "the land." For days my mind spun and my blood simmered until at once the Lord reminded me that "the boundary lines have fallen for me in pleasant places; indeed, I have a beautiful inheritance" (Ps. 16:6). What was a strip of property compared to depending on the lavish gifts of God where everything He deems important is mine and what He has promised is secure in Him (1 Cor. 3:20–23)? I'm not trivializing what we own or are given to steward, but it was a lesson among thousands in laying down my rights and trusting the Lord to protect whatever is truly mine.

As it turned out, my neighbor's documents proved more accurate than the lasers. I needed to take my fence in. But God had given me a gift in the process, a firm reality worth more than my yard: the only rights we as Christians have fall within the will of the Lord—that and no more—expressed Bonhoeffer.[13] And when we believe His will for our lives is more abundant and fulfilling than what we try to scrap for ourselves, freedom and joy abound.

In Christ's kingdom we are no longer a slave to our rights. After all, "The earth and everything in it, the world and its inhabitants, belong to the LORD" (Ps. 24:1). Those who humbly and resolutely wait for the kingdom of heaven to come in full will in the meantime find that everything is theirs in Christ.

Is there a "right" you need to surrender to Him? Is squabbling over what's "yours" eating up your precious time on earth? Place it in the Lord's hands and trust Him for all He desires to give you.

DAY 10

BLESSED ARE THE HUNGRY AND THIRSTY

"Blessed are those who hunger and thirst for righteousness, for they will be filled."

Matthew 5:6

I'VE DISCOVERED THAT BEING AN aunt is an exercise that falls somewhere between parenting and grandparenting. If you're too much like a parent, your nieces and nephews will leave you. If you acquiesce to their every whim like a grandparent, they'll run your life. We aunts walk a fine line.

When my niece Harper was nine, she went through a homemade lemonade kick. Wanting to encourage her culinary propensities, and apparently bereft of all good judgment, I got behind her efforts. On one occasion I walked into the kitchen where the faucet was running for the fun of it and Harper was slicing her lemons directly on my countertops, etching her mark with acidic drippings. In the middle of this costly experiment, I asked her to turn off the water she had ceased paying attention to. She respectfully and logically replied, "But why? It's free." And there commenced my long lesson on water scarcity, my monthly water bill, and probably world hunger issues.

Harper's concept of freely flowing water and readily available meals is not far from most of our own. Few of us in Western society have ever been without access to food or water. It's nearly impossible while living in an affluent culture to relate to the impoverished conditions of much of our world, not to mention first-century Palestine. For Jesus's followers, however, hungering and thirsting for righteousness would have been an easily accessible metaphor. The intensity with which a physical body yearns for water and food when bereft of it, a condition they knew, is the same intensity with which His listeners were to long for righteousness. Such people are the flourishing ones, Jesus says, because they will be satisfied to the fullest measure.

Jesus's first listeners, though, would have heard "hungering and thirsting for righteousness" differently than we hear it today. We tend to think of this in terms of the apostle Paul's later teachings about personal morality and the pursuit of holiness. Our minds may even race to the imputed righteousness of Christ given to us at salvation. While all of these aspects of righteousness are probably included in some way here, this fourth beatitude is tugging on the idea of *restorative justice*.[14] In other words, Jesus was addressing those whose hearts were aching for things to be put right in their domain—for the bad guys to be punished, the innocent to be protected, the powerful to no longer be allowed to oppress. Those who were longing for peace, love, and holiness to once again shape all of creation and pervade their broken world.[15]

You and I know this longing.

No one has to convince us our world is marred by sin, sickness, and death. The news is almost unbearable to watch or read anymore; mostly it's a highlight reel of all that's wrong with humanity. And in our personal lives, often the unjust get away scot-free while the honest and hardworking can't get a leg up. Injustice abounds. We know this in the depths of our beings. We can't escape the reality that we all live east of Eden, where little is fair, oppression is rampant, and outrage permeates the air. But we fool ourselves, don't we? We think that if we can just get this person to shape up, or when that better job finally comes through, or that new president gets in office, our world will be right again. But this is to hunger and thirst for a manageable comfortable life, not the enduring righteousness Jesus is speaking of.

So, instead of trying to satisfy our ravenous hunger with a different boyfriend, or slake our thirst with a new sofa, Jesus says to yearn for Him and the restoration His kingdom is already bringing about. Our highest calling as believers isn't to learn to manage our world's brokenness; nor is it to try to get through as comfortably or unscathed as possible. It's instead to settle for nothing less than God's pervasive, total, absolute restoration of our world and our hearts, His holiness to seep into the earth's crust, His Son Jesus to wholly reign with justice and goodness where evil is vanquished and peace flows without end.

If you will live your life toward that end, organizing it around all that God says in His Word is important for life and flourishing, Jesus promises: your craving for such a righteous world will one day be *filled*.

DAY 11

BLESSED ARE THE MERCIFUL

"Blessed are the merciful, for they will be shown mercy."

Matthew 5:7

THIS IS ONE OF THOSE "Jesus statements" that's easy to get on board with, at least theoretically. We wholeheartedly endorse the idea of showing mercy until someone really wrongs us, really has *done it this time*, and we're faced with reciprocating harm or showing mercy. Certainly Jesus doesn't expect me to pour out mercy in *this* situation, we think to ourselves—let's not be unreasonable.

Or perhaps our thoughts aren't so obvious a challenge to Jesus's words. We don't swing as far as unkind retaliation per se because, really, we're better Christians than that. But we may offer a feigned sort of mercy in public while gossiping about the person who hurt us in private. Or maybe we harbor unforgiveness toward them, or just point out one more time how badly they've messed up and how they really don't deserve our unmerited goodness. Obvious or subtle, there are so many ways to skirt the kind of mercy Jesus is speaking of here.

The most radical part of His statement, in light of the rest of His teachings, is that we are to show mercy to those who don't deserve it. This is precisely the challenge. I would so much rather show mercy to people who are worthy of it, who have earned it, those I happen to like. But if the tables are turned and *I* am the one in need of mercy, well, then, I hope it will be extended to me as an act of loving-kindness without cords of condemnation.

The word *mercy* here is much more than simply tolerating someone's behavior or passing over an offense. It beats with "concrete actions of love, compassion, sympathetic grace to those who are oppressed or to those who have sinned (cf. Gal. 6:1)."[16] It's more active than passive.

While we may need to show such action-packed goodness to those who have wronged us, mercy is also a virtue we get to show to those who are hurting, hungry, suffering injustice, or just downright in despair. Mercy's eyes are wide open, sensitive to the periphery, looking for those who could use a lift. Mercy can show up as a word of encouragement at the right time. It can come in the form of a bill paid or a meal shared or a vase of freshly cut flowers.

When I think of Jesus announcing this state of being as distinctly blessed in His kingdom, I wonder how that landed on His listeners. I imagine most of the crowd was aware of needing mercy for their wrongdoings, but they also may have needed a break from government oppressors and slack from landowners looking to settle balances. Did it sound crazy to the crowds, and perhaps even to the disciples, that the way to receive mercy was to give it, especially when they may have thought they had precious little to spare?

Here again is the upside-down way of the kingdom. When we show our offenders grace and offer practical kindness to the hurting and burdened, God promises to return it to us in our own hour of need. Most importantly, He will bestow it on judgment day.

This may feel like the opposite of mercy, like we have to earn mercy by showing it. Or worse yet, like something as exhausting as karma. But I think a better way of looking at it is that Jesus is describing the type of blessed life His true followers live. Those who have tasted God's extraordinary mercy will naturally be characterized by a merciful way of life. And when God's mercy has infiltrated us, is flowing out of us toward others, it can only mean that we are His children. And as children of our heavenly Father, when we most need mercy, it will be given us in fullest measure.

Jesus expounds on this later in Matthew's Gospel where He asks His disciples through a parable, "Shouldn't you also have had mercy on your fellow servant, as I had mercy on you?" (Matt. 18:33). So showing mercy is not about earning it; rather it's a result of God's gracious order. What He gives us, He wants us to give others.

Whom do you need to show mercy to? Who doesn't deserve it but needs it? Are your eyes of mercy open, alert to the needs around you? And are your feet moving toward such needs? This is the otherworldly mark of a person who has truly experienced the unmerited mercy of Christ, and this is what it means to live blessed.

DAY 12

BLESSED ARE THE PURE IN HEART

"Blessed are the pure in heart, for they will see God."

Matthew 5:8

One of the greatest gifts we've been given as humans is the gift of sight. What a sacred gift to behold the face of a loved one across the table at dinner. Or be mesmerized by joyful spells of snowflakes falling outside your window. I will never get over having marveled at the bleeding pink, red, and orange streaks an Amazonian sunset leaves behind. I have gazed at each of my nieces and nephews as fresh newborns, taking in their miniature noses, their gaping yawns, and every minuscule fingernail. So much of life's wonder is gathered with our eyes.

It is no surprise then that if Jesus is the image of the invisible God (Col. 1:15), the gift of having a pure heart is to see Him. What more could we hope to experience in our pursuit of holy living before God than to behold Him?

This brings up issues for us, though, because who considers himself or herself pure? We may be a lot of things—determined, courageous, hardworking, generous, perhaps even moral, but pure? We know ourselves too well to boast purity. For many of us, we feel so fundamentally impure that just the word brings up the sense of a ship having long since sailed leaving judgment in its wake.

But by virtue of Jesus's teaching that having a pure heart is a blessed way of life means it's a possible way of life. Purity is not out of reach for any of us!

It helps to understand purity in terms of being undivided or whole. This single-minded devotedness to God is a theme that runs throughout Jesus's Sermon. He is deeply concerned with our inward lives matching our outward lives and vice versa. He desires for us to be whole people whose desires, actions, and attitudes work together in the same direction in accordance with His good will. We don't have to live at war within ourselves.

Isn't this good news? Life in the kingdom of heaven is not about playacting, or faking it till we make it. It's not about performing on the outside while we die slow deaths on the inside because we know who we really are. No, it means that in His kingdom we're on our way from being a slave of unholy desires and harmful agendas to whole devotion to Christ.

It also means a life more meaningful than devoting an hour to Christ on Sundays, and perhaps a few other weekday moments, while living for our jobs, sports, shopping, movie watching, gaming, exercising, and *what are we going to eat next?* the rest of the week. Living with a pure heart means every part of our lives, secular and sacred, comes under the rule and reign of Jesus. In leisure and laughter, He is our joy. In trial and disappointment, He is our hope. In loneliness and grief, He is our fellowship. As we participate with God's grace, purging from our hearts the false gods of materialism, escape-filled entertainment, and workaholism, we will over time find darkness overtaken by light, the fog dispersed by the Morning Star. We will see God.

What is obscuring your vision of Him? Think about where your heart is divided, where your desires are tugging you away from the path of obedience, where an idol is so overgrown that you can barely see Jesus.

Dear reader, we know how impurity diminishes our view of Christ, the ways it encroaches on our ability to see Him, how it causes us to stumble aimlessly in darkness. Let us hold fast to Him today, the One who promises that if we confess our sins He is faithful and just to forgive and *purify* us from all unrighteousness (1 John 1:9).

Jesus, I want to see You. No pleasure or pastime, habit or secret is worth forfeiting my view of You. I confess what is keeping me divided in heart, what is keeping me from living the fullness of the blessed life You died to give me.

DAY 13

BLESSED ARE THE PEACEMAKERS

"Blessed are the peacemakers, for they will be called sons of God."

Matthew 5:9

I WONDER WHAT COMES TO mind when you hear the word *peacemaker*. I think of my soft and serene friends, the ones who rarely get ruffled, whose tongues are the seat of kind words. My imaginations may not be wrong but they are probably incomplete. "Blessed are the peacemakers" can feel cross-stitchy if we're not careful, like something one of our mom's friends would have given us to hang in our bedroom in the eighties—a reminder that Jesus would like us to be nice people. It turns out that peacemaking is about more than being nice, though this is never a bad reminder.

In the ancient Jewish world, peace (or *shalom,* as they would have known it), was a culturally rooted idea directly linked to the administration of justice and righteousness. It was a gift God gave His people when they lived under His reign and rule. But in first-century Palestine, peace was lacking. The Jews imagined it could only be restored through a powerful king and a strong military that could take back what was rightfully theirs.

Jesus had a different idea.

For Jesus, peacemaking has a lot to do with reconciliation. We are reconciled to God by Christ's blood and are given the ministry of reconciliation (2 Cor. 5:18). The dividing wall between Jews and Gentiles has been torn down so we can be one with God and with one another

(Eph. 2:14). Peace birthed from reconciliation is characterized by forgiveness and oneness. Perhaps the listeners on the hillside that day thought peace could only come if God kicked the bad guys out so the good guys could get back to being God's favored people. But Jesus ultimately brings peace by making "good" guys and "bad" guys one, transforming them both into His followers.

So, what does this mean for us today? All we have to do is think about our relationships to realize how hard being a peacemaker is. As I write, my feelings are hurt as a result of a long and painful situation, some of which could have been helped, some not. If left to my inclinations apart from Christ, I would like to take my ball and go home—my teammates can figure out how to shoot three-pointers without me (this is what Scripture refers to as my "sin nature" in case anyone is wondering). But here in the middle of potential division, Jesus's words firmly land. Peacemaking is meant to be enacted in the middle of our current circumstances—your marriage, or impossible work situation, or racial wound, or church split, or neighborhood squabble, or broken engagement. We are to pursue peace now in our real lives.

Peacemaking means participating with God in putting to death our pride and selfish agendas and desire to get back at someone. (Living under the control of these forces is precisely *not* the blessed life.) It may mean asking for forgiveness, or extending it. It may also mean standing up for someone who is being treated unjustly or wronged in the hopes that peace will prevail. It could mean "an active entrance into the middle of warring parties for the purpose of creating peace."[17] I wonder who has *that* cross-stitched and hanging on their walls?

Jesus explains that when our lives are about peace and reconciliation, we're testifying that we're "sons of God" because we're actively sharing in His character.[18] While the rest of the world is fighting for their rights, scrapping for what's theirs, the peacemakers are others centered and justice bound, seeking restoration and reconciliation. This is shalom. When God's people pursue it, we usher in the familiar but long-forgotten tastes of Eden to once again be enjoyed at our tables and in our world.

You and I can choose the way of peace today by humbling ourselves, admitting wrong, receiving an apology, fighting for justice, standing up for those being treated unfairly—or whatever other form peacemaking requires.

What step toward peace do you need to take? Will you move toward it today?

When you do, you will display the nature of God, the new nature He has given you as His child. You will taste shalom.

DAY 14

BLESSED ARE THOSE WHO ARE PERSECUTED

"Blessed are those who are persecuted because of righteousness, for the kingdom of heaven is theirs."

Matthew 5:10

This singular verse about persecution may have prompted my earlier distaste for the beatitudes. As a teenager and then young adult, I had a hard enough time not lurching toward all the world's sparkly offerings while also trying to be patient, humble, compassionate, and kind. Now I was supposed to try to get persecuted so I could inherit something I didn't really understand—the kingdom of heaven? I felt confused and discouraged. Having fun had a much more appealing ring to it.

As already mentioned, part of my problem was reading the Beatitudes as a list of to-do's so God would do this or that. In light of this assumption, how refreshing the words of one wonderful commentator about this passage: "The sermon, therefore, is not a list of requirements, but rather a description of the life of a people gathered by and around Jesus."[19] Once again, the Beatitudes are gifts much more than they are commands![20] They are realities more than they are obligations.

This may not solve all our problems, but it takes care of a big one. Jesus is not asking you to run around looking to get persecuted. He is declaring to you a new reality. And one of the new dimensions of His kingdom is that if you are suffering as a result of your righteousness toward God and faith in Jesus Christ, you are actually one of the flourishing ones. This goes against our natural sensibilities, and yet for those who have deeply suffered, you know that suffering is an invitation to fellowship with Christ. It's a bond that ties us to our Savior's side in a way that nothing else does. Suffering causes us to cozy up next to Him, nestling close enough to experience the power of His resurrection, yes, but also to share in the fellowship of His sufferings (Phil. 3:10). The apostle Paul would also write that just as Jesus's sufferings overflow into our lives so does God's comfort and compassion (2 Cor. 1:5).

It's impossible to have one without the other. Sharing in Jesus's sufferings means sharing in His consolation. Let that reality wash over you anew.

Now, even though the Beatitudes are not commands to be kept, per se, part of having faith in Jesus means we will experience some measure of hostility in this life—or in the case of many faithful believers in other parts of the world, even physical persecution. Since many of the values of our world are thoroughly at odds with the nature of God's kingdom, we're sure to experience backlash for our beliefs and the way we live our lives. In our Western culture, we generally don't put humility over pride, sacrifice before greed, or sacrificial love in place of lust. We're happy for everyone to do as they please as long as it doesn't "hurt" anyone, but everyone has a different idea of what it means to hurt others. To define things like good and evil, sin, sexuality, marriage, the equality of all people, or truth according to God's righteousness—and to *live* accordingly—is guaranteed to bring resistance. It's part of what it means to follow Jesus. Even Jesus Himself said that if the world hates us, it's only because it hated Him first (John 15:18).

But Jesus does not leave us here. His promise is that in our sufferings we possess the power and love and glory and hope of His kingdom. My Brazilian friend Sarah recently put it this way, "Suffering and hope are friends; it just sometimes takes a little while for them to learn to get along." So if walking in the ways of Christ has invited stone throwers and naysayers, or led you across the path of the spiteful, or caused you to lose someone or something dear to you, take heart. Jesus emphatically says to you, the kingdom is *yours*. Now in abundant measure and one day in full. Let your suffering's companion be the hope of Christ.

DAY 15

BLESSED ARE THE INSULTED

"You are blessed when they insult you and persecute you and falsely say every kind of evil against you because of me. Be glad and rejoice, because your reward is great in heaven. For that is how they persecuted the prophets who were before you."

Matthew 5:11–12

One of the reasons the Beatitudes have been difficult for me to grasp is because I continue to be committed to the poor theological idea that if I do what God wants me to do, life will work out mostly how I want it to. For those of us who are disappointed because we are still struggling or aching despite our acts of service and moral choices, we may be coming by our discouragement honestly. The Old Testament is filled with images of God's blessing committed people with lush and tangible gifts like flowing milk and honey, plump grapes, fine wheat, and rich wine. It's why we still talk about getting into "the promised land" after desert seasons of lost jobs, or hard marriages, or lonely singleness, or aching childlessness.

But notice Jesus's mention of the suffering prophets. They were spoken against and falsely accused and, worst of all, rejected not only by their enemies but also by their own people. The prophets were often in trouble for speaking God's saving truth to a people who didn't want to hear it. Ezekiel had to preach to Israel even after God said they would patently reject his message. A youth group shouted insults at Elisha and called him bald (little did they know how fashionable this would be one day). A king burned Jeremiah's scrolls, and eventually he was thrown into a cistern. The prophets had it hard, but they were God's beloved instruments.

Jesus gave His words about persecution while the curtain was closing on the Old Testament prophets and a new one was opening up on His followers who would ultimately form His church. Yes, Jesus was announcing a brand-new kingdom, a new way to live in community with others and Himself, and a new way to be human with soft hearts made malleable by His Spirit. But a thread from the past was being woven into the future—like the prophets who suffered for living out loud for the righteousness and justice of God, so Jesus's disciples would also encounter rejection, insults, even unspeakable persecutions at times. Dietrich Bonhoeffer understood this. He died in a concentration camp in Nazi Germany, having declared, "Suffering, then is the badge of true discipleship."[21]

This doesn't mean we're to race out and try to bring suffering upon ourselves. The reality is that being a Christ follower will naturally bring opposition. Trying to avoid it is like trying to pilot a plane without turbulence—it's part of the territory. So, if you're declaring Jesus as the one and only Savior of this world, if you treasure what He values—morally, ethically, materially—if you love God fully and your neighbor sacrificially, and if those things bring persecution upon you, Jesus says, *celebrate!* You've hit turbulence, which can only mean one thing: you're flying in the kingdom. Your path will not be obstacle free, but you're in the same lane as the prophets. You're in the best company, right in line with the heroes of the faith who came before you. And what's more, your reward is unimaginable, preserved for you in heaven.

I don't know what turbulence you've hit. I don't know what choices you've made on account of Jesus that have cost you. The rejection may feel like more than your heart can bear. But Jesus promises that when we suffer because of Him we have cause for rejoicing. Great is your reward to come. And great is your comfort and consolation now, for you are following in the footsteps of the prophets but also in the ones of the ultimate Prophet, your Savior, Jesus.

DAY 16

SALT OF THE EARTH

"You are the salt of the earth."

Matthew 5:13

I once spoke with an accomplished chef who said the only thing that sets great cooks apart is their ability to work with fat, citrus, and sodium. "Just use way more of each than you think and you'll be a top-tier cook," she explained. In laymen's terms, I think this means more butter, lemons, and salt. Despite her modesty, she's not wrong. Salt makes just about every dish more inspiring. I use it generously in my soups. My homemade loaves of bread cannot do without it. I have a friend who shakes it onto her tortilla chips like she needs them to experience blizzard conditions.

But for our first-century audience, salt was used for more than seasoning. It was a medicinal agent before the use of antibiotics. It was effective in removing stains. And with no electricity to power refrigerators, salt was essential for preservation. Rubbing it into raw fish, chicken, or beef cured it for future consumption. Perhaps this slowing down of decay was one of salt's most essential uses in the ancient world.

With this in mind, we can only imagine how Jesus's words must have landed on the ears of His disciples. They were to be a distinct community, a people different from the world for the world. But how could this be when all Jesus had to work with were the poor in spirit, the persecuted, the trampled, those "whose only weapon is purity of heart"?[22] How could it be that those who would preserve culture and society were the peacemakers, the merciful, those who hungered and thirsted for righteousness? It must have seemed outlandish to those on the hillside that day.

Maybe it feels outlandish to us now.

When Jesus calls His followers to be the salt of the earth, He means we're to be a flavorful people, known by our love for others, our humility, our moral goodness, and sometimes for speaking the truth with loving-kindness. We are to be healing people, pressing Christ's cleansing power into the deep wounds of those around us in a way that momentarily stings but eternally heals. And perhaps most significantly, we are to be people of preservation. Our deeds should be salty enough to slow down the evil in this world, arresting the decay caused by cruelty, greed, oppression, poverty, and so many other forms of deprivation.

And when Jesus said "you" are the salt of the earth, He wasn't saying His disciples were an option among many; rather He was saying, "'You and only you' are the earth's salt and the world's light."[23] What does this mean? It means that the church is His agent of redemption for this world and there is no Plan B. We're not meant to operate in isolation as our own individual grains, doing our own thing; rather we're to make up a flavorful, healing, and preserving *community* under the name of Christ. Being the salt of the earth means nothing is more relevant to this world than His people, the church, joined in unity working for the common good.

I wonder what resources you have to share that might slow down the decay in someone's life. Perhaps you have wisdom that can be rubbed into the deep wounds of a soul who has lost his or her way. Maybe God has given you the gift of helping, teaching, organizing, counseling, or leading, and it's time to use those gifts to flavor a bland society weary of doing the same self-centered activities over and over with the same disappointing results. Who can say it better than John Stott: "Christian salt has no business to remain snugly in elegant little ecclesiastical salt cellars; our place is to be rubbed into the secular community."[24]

Who can you be salt for today? Someone needs the healing, flavor, and preservation that only a heaping spoon of Christian salt can bring.

DAY 17

REMAINING SALTY

"But if the salt should lose its taste, how can it be made salty? It's no longer good for anything but to be thrown out and trampled under people's feet."

Matthew 5:13

Every year after Christmas our neighborhood casts off our Christmas trees on the grounds of a local park. Eventually the trees get pushed through a wood chipper, and the mulch is used to line the trails. I love my January walks there, where the last vestige of Christmas pine hangs in the air. But eventually the scent fades, and the charming trees that once adorned our homes are now only good to provide traction under muddy soles. Perhaps a little like the unsalty salt Jesus speaks of here.

After He surprisingly declared to his small group of everyday disciples that they were the salt of the earth, the ones who would go on to impact the world in profound ways, He gave a warning. Salt should maintain its pizzazz because it can't be made tasty again; if it loses its vitality, it's only good for people to trample on. If we as the church are to be careful to maintain our saltiness, we need to know how it can be lost.

Interestingly, salt is a stable compound that can't actually lose its saltness.[25] Without refineries in ancient Palestine, salt from the Dead Sea was often mixed with sediment and debris.[26] It looked like salt, but it didn't have the power or punch of salt because it was a contaminated mixture. So perhaps Jesus's metaphor isn't about salt losing its inherent qualities but about it being combined with other ingredients that weaken its taste and effectiveness. In other words, we as the church lose our saltiness when we try to blend a little of the world with a little of Jesus. We grow lackluster when we try to follow Christ while also indulging passions and desires that lead away from His heart.

Not blending in with the world has been one of the greatest challenges for me, especially when I was younger. I loved Jesus and desired to follow Him, but boy did I love a lot of other competing things. Christ's sanctifying power is to this day purging the impurities in my life so what is left is more and more of Him. I know this is true for you, too.

How we long to be salty with His love.

When we looked at the beatitude of purity, we learned that having a whole, undivided heart for Christ is a theme running throughout the Sermon. It shows up again here in Jesus's call for His people to be distinct from the world around them so as to be agents of change. For salt to be effective it must be pure and uncontaminated. Once again, Jesus's unknown band of disciples couldn't have possibly expected Him to declare them radical instruments of redemption in the world. Wouldn't this distinction be reserved for the religious elite, the temple, the Torah, the city of Jerusalem?[27] We think along similar lines today. If the world is really going to change, won't it be through more education, scientific advancement, and the wealthy eliminating poverty? These are helpful aids, but true and enduring change can only come through the people of God sold out to Him as salty Christ followers.

To be the salt of the earth is to be a people in Christ's fellowship. It's being serious about the declining state of the world so we can be serious about arresting its decay as contributors toward its healing. It's taking inventory of our own hearts and seeing where our saltiness has lost its edge, not because Jesus has become less but because our hearts are committed to lesser things. It's seeing where we've tried to combine our worldly loves with our first love, leaving us bland and ineffective. What a moment in time to wake up and be the people of God to the world He's called us to serve. In the words of John Stott, "You must be what you are. You are salt, and so you must retain your saltness and not lose your Christian tang."[28]

Dear Father, let us not be uninteresting chameleons who change with the culture's colors. Help us be distinct, flavorful, and full of Your tang offering the world a taste of Your love.

DAY 18

LIGHT OF THE WORLD

"You are the light of the world. A city situated on a hill cannot be hidden. No one lights a lamp and puts it under a basket, but rather on a lampstand, and it gives light for all who are in the house. In the same way, let your light shine before others, so that they may see your good works and give glory to your Father in heaven."

Matthew 5:14–16

At three years old I toddled up and down the sidewalk singing "This Little Light of Mine" for anyone who cared to listen to its rich and poetic lyrics. "Hide it under a bushel? No!" was my favorite line, despite not knowing what a bushel was or what kind of light I was supposed to be holding forth. And I had no idea I was singing a portion of Jesus's most famous message. (I'm still memorizing and singing truths I'm having to grow into.) Familiarity with something can sometimes cloak its message, though, and what a message this is!

First, we must think of being the light of the world as running parallel to being the salt of the earth. The metaphors are meant to be digested side by side. We really could use an extra stanza, "This little salt of mine, I'm gonna let it stay salty" so we can get both images together in the same song. Perhaps someone can get to work on this. Both salt and light are agents of impact, both give and expend themselves, both are distinct from their surroundings![29] Perhaps one of the differences between the two is that salt has defensive qualities that restrain evil, while light is on the offense dispelling darkness.[30]

In verse 16 Jesus explains exactly how this proactive light expresses itself: it will shine through our good works. In my younger years this felt like a chore; today it feels like *what more could we possibly want God's kingdom to be known for?* Jesus makes plain that our love for others is through practical, tangible, life-giving, light-giving deeds that are visible. The people around us will benefit from our love and care for them. They will notice. However, we won't do such kind and sacrificial things so people will applaud us—Jesus will soon get to this misinterpretation—rather, so everyone's attention will turn to the goodness of our heavenly Father and they will give Him glory.

Yes, this may mean reordering some of our priorities. It may mean decisive shifts in how we spend our time, but it also may mean simply being aware that every encounter, the tone of our voice, the genuine inquiry to a coworker, *How are you?* can shine Christ in our world.

My house is currently under construction, and I have a dumpster in my backyard. (If you want to make friends and influence people, get a dumpster. I am presently the most sought-after human in the neighborhood.) A few neighbors asked if they could pay me to toss their basement junk in my unusually large trash can. It occurred to me that letting them freely unload their unwanted items was a small way to be of help, to hold forth my light. I realize that in terms of shining lights this act registers as barely flickering, but I hope small gestures of warmth like this one will open up future opportunities to share the brighter light of God's redemption, forgiveness, and beauty. We have to start somewhere.

What encouraging truth do you have to speak? What beautiful gift might you give? What good might you do? You have no idea what darkness you might be pushing back in a person's life, what hope you might be offering at just the right moment.

Jesus makes clear that our light is to be abundantly practical. As practical as a lamp . . . or a dumpster. So, yes, we want to live distinct lives that shine bright because of personal holiness, but we also want to live lives characterized by proactive good works on behalf of those around us. And when we hold forth our candles alongside others in the body of Christ, which is exactly how Jesus meant His message to be embodied, the blaze will be so great it will be as visible, as distinctly unmistakable, as an entire city on a hill hearkening to all who are weary of sitting in darkness.

DAY 19

LIGHT THAT REFLECTS UPON OUR FATHER

"You are the light of the world. A city situated on a hill cannot be hidden. No one lights a lamp and puts it under a basket, but rather on a lampstand, and it gives light for all who are in the house. In the same way, let your light shine before others, so that they may see your good works and give glory to your Father in heaven."

Matthew 5:14–16

With all the activity going on in our lives—the email inbox that needs responses, the front beds that need weeding, the kids' games—perhaps the thought of shining a light consisting of visible acts of goodness sounds tiring to you, one more out-of-reach task on the list. Consider me an empathetic soul, one who often needs to be reminded that Christ is the source of light for our world (John 8:12). Meaning, you and I don't have to manufacture the light; we need only hold it forth as His church through active love as we go about our days. And where the song gets it wrong, Satan can't blow it out.

The Jews listening to Jesus that day would have understood the glow and beauty of biblical light as rooted in the Old Testament, especially Isaiah, where it has a lot to do with "knowledge, truth, revelation, and love."[31] So when Jesus speaks in terms of the church being known for her visible, tangible good works, He is doing so with these themes in mind. This is important for us modern-day torchbearers because we want to be careful that we're not holding forth lights of moralism. To be clear, moral goodness is essential to holiness; we cannot do without it. But we must take care that our warm and inviting lights don't turn into judgmental torches that burn people instead of warm them and light their way. This is not to say that the flames of meekness, peacemaking, hungering for justice, purity, and so forth won't mean people aren't upset with us sometimes. The beatitude of persecution means part of the Christian's journey will be met with resistance. But our collective light should be one that reveals the goodness of the gospel, teaches the blessed life according to God's Word, and reflects the knowledge and truth of Jesus. Always with love.

I wonder, dear Christ follower, how your action-packed deeds can express the light of these qualities to those around you in both big and small ways. Because Jesus takes pains to state the obvious: people don't turn on lamps only to cover them, and a lit-up city on a hill is impossible to hide.

I think the idea here is that you and I are prone to hiding our lights. Maybe not under a bushel but under cloaks of fear and rejection—What will people think of us if we love them in the name of Jesus? Sometimes our laziness dims our light—we're simply too committed to our comforts and entertainment to sacrifice for others. *We just need a night at home in front of a good movie!* What about judgmentalism? How many times have we withheld our light from those we think don't deserve it? Pride, unforgiveness, greed . . . can also keep us from actively loving others, from keeping our candles burning.

"It is one thing to stop the spread of evil; it is another to promote the spread of truth, beauty and goodness."[32] If our salt is to remain salty, our light must continue to shine. And as salt holds back decay, light penetrates the darkness. So we ask ourselves, What is obscuring our light before our neighbors, coworkers, relatives? And what heart posture or behavior is keeping the lamp that illumines our closest relationships from being able to "give light for all who are in the house"?

Today, may we carry the light of Christ that shone before creation and burns without end.

DAY 20

JESUS, THE FULFILLMENT OF THE LAW

"Don't think I came to abolish the Law or the Prophets. I did not come to abolish but to fulfill. For truly I tell you, until heaven and earth pass away, not the smallest letter or one stroke of a letter will pass away from the law until all things are accomplished."

Matthew 5:17–18

Imagine you are on the hillside with Jesus's disciples listening to His teaching. Your heart has been refreshed by the Beatitudes, and you've been given the enormous, undeserved privilege of being salt and light in the world. You then hear Jesus say that He hasn't come to abolish the Law or the Prophets (shorthand for the Old Testament). You whisper to your friend, *What did He just say?* because you think you must have missed something. The statement feels out of place. Why mention that now?

Apparently, Jesus's teaching that the poor in spirit would inherit the kingdom and a handful of non-elite, Palestinian peasants would be the ones to change the entire world must have seemed off-putting to some. Perhaps even heretical. Here Jesus is making clear that He is fully in line with the Old Testament. His teaching is radical, but it's not unhinged from all God has been doing through His people since Abraham. (One of Matthew's great aims is to show how Jesus is fully rooted in the Law of Moses and is the One about whom the prophets spoke.)

But Jesus goes a step further, or maybe I should say a massive leap further. Not only has He *not* come to abolish the teachings and message of the Old Testament, but He *has* come to fulfill it (fill it up to completion). Not even the most committed Jew would ever claim such a thing. Everyone knew only God was capable of this kind of perfection. Jesus's statement here is the linchpin of the New Testament. Everything hangs on this proclamation. If Jesus is wrong, this is pure blasphemy, but if He's right, He's the Messiah who has come to save us.

Today we question Jesus's authority for different reasons than perhaps the Jews on the hillside that day. Most aren't hung up on whether Jesus is after the order of the Old Testament as much as they wonder about other things—was He just another prophet, a sage, a respected religious figure among many? Does He have any relevance to our lives today? Is He really God?

Perhaps these questions are fully settled in your heart. You believe that Jesus is Lord, King, and God Himself. But maybe it's been a while since you've let His words meet your weary and striving soul in its failed attempts at fulfilling its own righteousness.

What a wonderful time to pause and consider His fulfilling the Law. Where you have failed, perhaps for the seventieth or hundred and seventieth time, Jesus has accomplished the demands of His rules of righteousness *for you*. Where you cannot get a grip on your sexual desires, He has come to restore them. Where all the self-help books and seminars have fallen short, and your inner truth has become more truth about yourself than you can actually bear, He is your righteousness. Where the sacrificial lambs, Torah observance, temple rituals, yearly feasts of the Old Testament failed to achieve wholeness for the Jew, and where our modern-day attempts to *do better next time*, find a new therapist, or be a better person have failed to ultimately fix us, Jesus says, *It is finished. Not a stroke of the Law has been missed. I am the end of the whole thing. All the Old Testament demanded and predicted has been filled up in My person. Receive it. Receive Me.*

This is the part in Jesus's Sermon where we realize the Christian life isn't primarily about what we do but whose we are. How we live matters, but this will be an outpouring of what Christ has wholly accomplished for us. So simply pause for a minute and receive. Cease striving, and fall back into the arms of a Savior who has fulfilled every demand of God's Law, once and for all, for you.

DAY 21

THE SACRED LAW

"Therefore, whoever breaks one of the least of these commands and teaches others to do the same will be called least in the kingdom of heaven. But whoever does and teaches these commands will be called great in the kingdom of heaven."

Matthew 5:19

If we want to know what we value, what's important to us, we need only look as far as our daily schedule. For the most part, we tend to organize our lives around what matters to us. Some of us build our calendar around our diet and workout regimen. When can we get to the gym? When will we meal-plan? For others, it's all around our children's activities, or our career, or our leisure endeavors. How fast can we get to the golf course or the mall or our favorite show? For still others, it's church programs. We reserve a certain night of the week for Bible study, plan our summer trips around vacation Bible school, and make sure Sundays are set apart for worship.

For committed Jews, the central and organizing factor for all of life was the Torah—God's revealed, life-giving Law about who He is and how His people are to live. For them, it stood at the center of everything.

As we looked at yesterday, what a shock it was when Jesus declared that He was the Law's fulfillment. Plainly speaking, He was saying that "following him means following the Torah."[33] This was a radical shift in thinking for Jesus's disciples and the listening crowds. Radical, because until that point the Jewish people had tried to follow the Law the best they could, some more intent about it than others. But now Jesus was teaching that His disciples needed to shift their focus from being Law keepers to Christ followers. By doing the latter, the former would take care of itself. Following Jesus didn't mean doing away with the Law; in fact, Jesus stated the opposite—the greatest in the kingdom will be those who not only act according to the Law but also pass its goodness onto others by teaching it.

I think if we're honest, most of us don't know what to make of this passage any more than the disciples and crowds did when Jesus first spoke it. We're not sure how Jesus has fulfilled the Law for us while still maintaining we must live by it in order to be residents of His kingdom. Dietrich Bonhoeffer helps us out here. "The righteousness is therefore not a duty owed, but a perfect and truly personal communion with God."[34]

It's that "not a duty owed" part that stands out for us. We don't live by God's commands because we're trying to earn salvation, or attempting to tip the scales further in the direction of good works instead of questionable ones, or arm-wrestling God into giving us what we want. We live by and teach His commands because this is the good life! It's the way we enter into "a perfect and truly personal communion with God."

This is why Jesus says don't "break" (or relax) even the tiniest of laws. It's that serious because His Word is life. This is an especially needed word for us living in a post-Christian culture. Where the Jews may have thought they could keep the law by extreme effort, we wonder if we need to keep it at all. Where many around us have no use or regard for God's commands, it's easy for us to relax His law here or there and still feel like we're ahead of most of the people we know. We don't often think about how the extra drink, or occasional sex with our boyfriend or girlfriend, or gossip, or greed, or pride will interfere with our communion with Christ, as much as we think about the pleasures we're missing out on. But this is to miss the privilege, the plain novelty of what "greatness" looks like in God's kingdom.

What part of God's law are you relaxing, cutting corners on, or simply not obeying? This is a high-stakes question. We won't keep the law perfectly, nor can we—Jesus's beloved disciple, John, understood this well (1 John 2:1). But, according to Jesus, His true followers will care deeply about what matters to the heart and ways of God. Our motivation to keep His commands won't be out of religious duty but because Jesus has made it possible for us to live the good life with Him in His kingdom.

Bonhoeffer finishes his earlier quote by reminding us that "Jesus not only possesses this righteousness, but is himself the personal embodiment of it. He *is* the righteousness of the disciples."[35] His righteousness *in you* empowers you to live by His commands and pass them onto others. And as John encourages, "His commands are not burdensome" (1 John 5:3 NIV).

Dear friend, Jesus paid the ultimate price to fulfill the Law so we could live by its blessing, fullness, and truth. How can we settle for anything less?

DAY 22

A GREATER RIGHTEOUSNESS

"For I tell you, unless your righteousness surpasses that of the scribes and Pharisees, you will never get into the kingdom of heaven."

Matthew 5:20

Sit with this verse for a moment. How does it make you feel? Taken all by itself, I find it to be one of the more frightful and shocking verses in Jesus's Sermon. In our modern day, the term *Pharisee* can be shorthand for hypocrite or judgmental religious person. But in its own day, the Pharisees were the pinnacle examples of what it meant to be a student and keeper of God's Word, and the scribes were meticulous in their adherence to it. For Jesus to say that our righteousness must exceed theirs seems to be a game-over statement for those of us without a blemish-free track record.

Here we had our hopes up about being salt and light and Jesus fulfilling the Law for us, and suddenly it appears we're disqualified.

When my nephew Will was four, his first introduction to Little League soccer coincided with the World Cup. He seemed to enjoy his practices but was nearly brought to tears over the thought of playing in a game. My brother David and his wife Megen couldn't get to the bottom of his anxiety. One day while the World Cup was airing on television, Will pointed to the overflowing stadium that was roaring and raucous. With lips trembling he said, "I'm not ready for that." Will thought he was going from Little League practices to a match on the world stage in Barcelona. This was going to be easy to clarify.

This is the leap it feels like Jesus is asking His disciples to make. They're the fishermen-types who are new to following Christ, certainly nowhere near the top of the Jewish religious heap, and suddenly Jesus is requiring from them World Cup holiness. How ever will their righteousness exceed that of the professional holy people? And how ever will ours? This is not a verse we can afford to skirt or leave in the *things in life that are vague* category. Our life in God's kingdom depends on it.

John Stott is so helpful when he writes, "Christian righteousness far surpasses pharisaic righteousness in kind rather than in degree."[36] In other words, exceeding the Pharisees' righteousness doesn't mean that if they got a 96 percent on their law-keeping score we'll need a 97 percent to squeak into the kingdom (degree). It means that the righteousness that pleases Jesus is that which springs from a pure heart (kind). Jesus desires that our outward actions match the inward state of our hearts. If He went after anyone in the Gospels, it was the religious leaders for doing the right things with the wrong hearts.

So, how do we get this new kind of righteousness? The prophet Jeremiah spoke of a coming day when God would write His law on our hearts (Jer. 31:33), and similarly, Ezekiel said our hearts of stone would be made into hearts of flesh, and God's Spirit would live within us (Ezek. 36:26). We must see Jesus's words in light of these prophecies. For the morally exhausted, for those who have managed to pull it together outwardly but whose hearts are cold inwardly, World Cup holiness isn't about beating the religious leaders at their own game; it's about receiving an altogether new kind of righteousness, the kind that only comes from a new heart.

The type of righteousness Jesus demands is the type He gives.

So, today, receive from His hand. Ask for a soft heart of flesh, an awareness of His teaching written on your heart, and fellowship with the Spirit living inside you. Take seriously His statement that your righteousness *must* exceed that of the religious leaders. And then go live in the way of the righteousness Jesus delights to give you.

DAY 23

CUTTING THE ROOT OF ANGER

"You have heard that it was said to our ancestors, 'Do not murder,' and whoever murders will be subject to judgment. But I tell you, everyone who is angry with his brother or sister will be subject to judgment. Whoever insults his brother or sister will be subject to the court. Whoever says, 'You fool!' will be subject to hellfire."

Matthew 5:21–22

I HATE TO ADMIT IT, but of all the negative emotions at a person's disposal, anger was one that came easily to me, especially when I was younger. I can still get pretty worked up about things that others might get teary over, stuff down, or shrug off altogether. (I have always wanted to be more like the shruggers, the ones who know how to let things roll off their backs in maddening circumstances.) So today's passage is a bit problematic for me, partially because Jesus puts anger on par with murder, and that just isn't good news. At least not on the surface. But we'll get to that in a minute.

Yesterday we talked about having a "greater righteousness" that flows from the heart. We're entering a new section of Jesus's Sermon (5:21–48) where Jesus will help us understand what this type of righteousness looks like in our real, everyday lives. He is about to get extremely practical. He will take six commands from the law, ones familiar to the Jews, and correctly define them. Never had anyone on the hillside heard the law taught the way Jesus was about to teach it. What many understood as simply behavioral rules to keep—like don't murder someone when you're mad at them—Jesus taught as windows that exposed the true condition of our hearts.

For example, if you're angry at someone but you haven't killed them, well done. But if you're composing in your mind a nasty social media post about that person, that's no good. In fact, rage toward a brother or sister, slandering them, or calling them a fool is worthy of the same kind of judgment as murder: hellfire. (I do wish there was a pleasanter way to get this across.) The good news here is that, despite its seriousness, Jesus's interpretation of the Old Testament law is that God cares deeply about how we treat one another.

It's not okay to be clear of murder while nursing hatred in our hearts toward someone, fantasizing about their downfall, or insulting their character or intelligence. Again, and we will continue to return to this, Jesus isn't solely interested in our outward moral behaviors but about our *entire hearts* being formed in His image. He wants our insides to match our outsides and for His followers to genuinely love one another. This has always been the case. While we tend to look at the Old Testament as law and the New Testament as love, they're not at odds with each other. Law and love go together. Not to mention, much of the prophets' messaging was about repentance that flows from a pure heart.[37] Jesus isn't upping the ante on anger, or raising the bar; rather He's revealing what the true purpose of the law's *do not murder* was from the beginning—that we would love people from our hearts, so much so that not even anger will find a home within us.

If we find ourselves lashing out with a harsh word at a friend, coworker, spouse, or child, it's time to acknowledge, *Lord, my heart needs Your tending.* If a record of wrongs is playing on repeat in our minds, we must deal with the anger swirling inside us. While it's difficult to acknowledge that anger and harmful words are right up there with murder, the flip side is that this expresses the high value Jesus places on human relationships. How uninspiring would life in the kingdom be if anything goes as long as we don't kill one another? Jesus has come for so much more than this, to restore relationships and cause them to abound in love. He wants full-scale flourishing in our communities, not half-hearted attempts at coexisting next to a person we secretly can't stand.

We can't love one another well when slander is on the tip of our tongue or anger is festering beneath the surface. Jesus said, *You've heard it said don't murder, but that's just the beginning*. . . . Are you hanging on to someone's list of offenses? A person to whom you need to show grace instead of frustration? Anger is a predictable thief of the blessed life. Don't let it steal another moment of peace or the joy of a reconciled relationship.

DAY 24

GO AND RECONCILE

"So if you are offering your gift on the altar, and there you remember that your brother or sister has something against you, leave your gift there in front of the altar. First go and be reconciled with your brother or sister, and then come and offer your gift. Reach a settlement quickly with your adversary while you're on the way with him to the court, or your adversary will hand you over to the judge, and the judge to the officer, and you will be thrown into prison. Truly I tell you, you will never get out of there until you have paid the last penny."

Matthew 5:23–26

Where would we be without the people most precious to us, our family members and best friends? Or how would we get along without our church communities made up of soup makers, construction workers, elementary school teachers, financial advisors ready to lend a hand? Even our extended communities and support systems help keep us tethered in an unstable world. New neighbors recently moved in next door to me, and we've already exchanged flowers and chocolate-covered pretzels, small gestures left on each other's front porches that say "hello" and "I hope to know you soon." As the wonderful Reuben Welch wrote in his book, *We Really Do Need Each Other*.[38]

It's for the sake of relationships that Jesus uses such strong words about murder, anger, and words that cut to a person's core, and the reason He says that if a brother or sister has something against you, drop your gift at the altar like a hot potato and run to their homes to make amends. His urging is all about the importance of close-knit community and restored relationships.

In ancient times, offering your gift (probably an animal sacrifice) at the altar was a sacred and rare occasion that meant journeying to the temple in Jerusalem.[39] From Galilee, where Jesus was teaching His disciples, this was about an eighty-mile journey south. You can imagine the astounding inconvenience of leaving your sacrifice at the altar, huffing it back home to apologize or get some group counseling, returning to the temple to offer your sacrifice, then journeying home once again. The illustration seems a bit over the top, which is exactly how Jesus wanted it to come across.[40] Our worship and sacrifices aren't pleasing to God when we know we've wounded someone but haven't tried to make amends, in particular with a brother or sister in Christ.

Jesus's second illustration is similar in its urgency for reconciliation, but this time the scenario doesn't take place within the church but in a court of law. Jesus isn't giving legal advice here; rather He is urging us to make amends with our adversaries when possible and not allow strained relationships to drag on. Both situations require the Christ follower to do whatever he or she can to restore communion whether with another believer or someone outside the body of Christ.

It's important to reassure those who have been abused or abandoned or sorely wounded that not all relationships can or should be restored. Jesus's words are meant to be taken as a general teaching on the importance of seeking restoration, especially when we've hurt someone. (Notice Jesus doesn't say leave your gift at the altar if *you* have something against someone but if *they* have something against you.) Whether actual restoration happens or not, we should do what is reasonably possible. And where restoration isn't achievable, we must take great care that our hearts aren't eaten up with cancerous bitterness.

Perhaps there's a gnawing in your spirit, someone you know you've offended, maybe even deeply wounded. Jesus says, *Go*. That tiny word expresses a world of redemptive movement toward a person made in God's image. Going may mean a text, a call, a written letter, a scheduled coffee. . . . *Hey, it's me. Can we talk?*

Jesus then tells us to be *reconciled*. It's one of the most glorious words in Scripture made possible through Jesus's reconciling us to God. And while there is no guarantee that all will be resolved, you will have loved the other person the way Jesus commands, having expressed the goodness of God's kingdom here on earth. And this is no small matter because "nothing expresses kingdom realities more than reconciled relations."[41]

Is there someone you need to make amends with? Someone you know you've offended? Make plans to reach out with kindness and grace—this is your part. You can then trust the reconciliation part to your heavenly Father.

DAY 25

LOVING PEOPLE FROM THE HEART

"You have heard that it was said, 'Do not commit adultery.' But I tell you, everyone who looks at a woman lustfully has already committed adultery with her in his heart."

Matthew 5:27–28

We can barely read or watch the news without witnessing how wayward sexual desires thoroughly crush the hearts of men and women, often leaving children in their devastating aftermath. The shattering nature of adultery makes it an especially damaging sin to ourselves, our relationships, and our communion with God. What starts in the heart, and so quietly moves to the imagination, can turn into seemingly innocent gestures that if not radically cut off can lead to adultery and the loss of all we hold dear.

Forgiveness and restoration through Jesus are ever present for the adulterer. No sin committed is outside the realm of our repentance or the reach of His grace. But piecing back together the life that existed before adultery is impossible. So inestimable is its cost that Jesus says it's not good enough to not commit it outwardly; we've got to get at the root of it—we're not even to lust. It may seem as if Jesus is nitpicking here until we consider that lust turns a person made in the image of God into an object whose sole purpose is to entertain our thoughts or quell our loneliness. Lust may seem others focused, but it is always me centered and simply not the abundant life Jesus longs to give us.

Moreover, lust at its core is a lack of trust in God's ability to fulfill our needs and satisfy our desires. When we foster sexual thoughts about someone we're not married to, it often comes down to this: we don't believe God knows what He's talking about. Dietrich Bonhoeffer put it this way: "Lust is impure because it is unbelief, and therefore it is to be shunned."[42]

Like Adam and Eve in the garden, we're convinced God is withholding from us. He can't possibly mean for me as a single woman to abstain from sex apart from getting married and, on top of that challenging existence, not to even fantasize about it. Or, if you're married, He can't possibly mean that you're never to let your imagination dwell on the ways some other man or woman might make you so much happier than your spouse does or might take away the loneliness you don't think you can bear any longer. Trusting God is never more difficult than when it means going against our fallen desires.

But Jesus is not holding out on you. He is relentless in His pursuit to give you life, like springs of living water bubbling from within you.

Whereas lust stirs up our desire for what will gnaw away at our conscience, our soul rest, our peace, our sleep, our work, our relationships, Jesus has come that we might have life that cannot be taken from us! Participating in this full life means saying no to anything we fancy that opposes His heart, and this is the challenging part, especially when it comes to our sexual natures. It means trusting that His ways are better than the ones that presently *feel* so much better to us.

King David said that God's commands were to him sweeter than honey dripping from a honeycomb (Ps. 19:9–10). When I was younger, I didn't understand this. Some of His commands tasted like meatloaf with minced onions, which was a real chore for me to eat when my mom served it for dinner. It may at first seem bitter to dwell on good and righteous things instead of letting our sexual desires run away with our thoughts, or breaking off an illicit relationship that's heading (or has already gone) down a disastrous path. Dying to our fallen desires and retraining our thought patterns in the ways of Jesus is hard work. But as the seeds of our obedient choices germinate beneath the soil, punch their fists above the ground, and sprout up to bear the fruit of godly choices, we will recall with deep affection the psalmist's words—his commands are simply delicious.

The Lord has life for you today. Lust is a villainous impostor of love, a devastating counterfeit. God's ways are not meant to take from you but to give to you. Replace lustful thoughts with life-giving ones. Make no provision for adultery or anything that could even lead in that direction. Jesus is telling you the truth, and He *cannot* withhold from you.

DAY 26

BE RUTHLESS WITH YOUR SIN

"If your right eye causes you to sin, gouge it out and throw it away. For it is better that you lose one of the parts of your body than for your whole body to be thrown into hell. And if your right hand causes you to sin, cut it off and throw it away. For it is better that you lose one of the parts of your body than for your whole body to go into hell."

Matthew 5:29–30

Oh, the folly of attempting to write a lighthearted, feel-good devotional based on Jesus's Sermon on the Mount. I understand that most people read their devotionals first thing in the morning, hoping to sip on encouraging words from Scripture as if it were freshly brewed coffee. I apologize for instead dousing you with cold water. But since we're taking the long view here, we can welcome Jesus's ice bath as a gift that will hopefully jar us awake to the reality of our sin so we can live the life that is truly life.

I think the tendency with today's passage is to take Jesus's metaphor too far or not far enough. On the "too far" end are those who take literally what Jesus certainly meant as a metaphor. On the "not far enough" end are those who determine that this is only a passage about our inability to meet the demands of the law and therefore need a Savior. In other words, Jesus doesn't mean for us to *do* anything here. While it's certainly true we need Jesus's saving grace, if we keep to the immediate context, Jesus has just referenced Old Testament laws such as "don't murder" and "don't commit adultery" where He probed beneath each one looking for anger here or traces of lust there. His remedy is decisive—cut out whatever in your life is causing sin's disease. So, yes, there is something for us to *do.*

I remember reading through a scholar's commentary on these verses while on a plane returning to Nashville. I set my book on my lap and took a break to catch up on the news. One of the headlines caught my attention. It was something along the lines of "Man without Arms Stabs Woman with His Feet." The gist was that this person had figured out how to hold a knife between his toes and from a spot on a street corner wounded a woman who was walking by. After having just been studying today's passage, the takeaway for me was immediate—even if we remove the parts of our body that are most active in sin, we'd find another part ready to make itself useful. Why? Because sin springs from the heart (Matt. 5:19).

Jesus's potent metaphor teaches us to radically eliminate what is causing us to sin. Thankfully, this won't mean gouging out an eye or sawing off a limb, but it might mean breaking ties to an adulterous relationship, striking the Internet from our phones, cutting out alcohol or foods that make us sluggish and irritable, or taking a long break from social media, which constantly reminds us of what we don't have. Only the Holy Spirit can testify with our own spirits about how this will look in our lives.

So, dear reader, the good news we need to hear today is not only that Jesus has met the demands of God's law in our place, giving us "salvation when we die" but also that His grace goes further still, empowering us to live right here and now with "greater righteousness." Dallas Willard puts it this way: "We consume the most grace by leading a holy life."[43] Let's consume the grace necessary to put to death the deeds of our selfish natures (Col. 3:5–11) so we can walk according to Jesus's ways and teachings. For His grace gives us the power to participate with Him in cutting out the sins that don't serve us in His kingdom. His grace transforms our hearts so our actual deeds will change, too. It's where the cold water starts to feel really refreshing on our skin because it reminds us that we're alive to the life He's come to give us.

DAY 27

THE GIFT OF MARRIAGE

"It was also said, 'Whoever divorces his wife must give her a written notice of divorce.' But I tell you, everyone who divorces his wife, except in a case of sexual immorality, causes her to commit adultery. And whoever marries a divorced woman commits adultery."

Matthew 5:31–32

Most everyone has been touched by divorce in some way. Perhaps you're a child of divorced parents, the mother or father of a divorced adult child, a spouse who's been left against your will, or one who filed for divorce because of unsafe circumstances or marital infidelity. Perhaps you're on the other side of a divorce that you would even say was mostly your fault. As we receive Jesus's teachings on marriage and divorce (He expounds on the topic more in Matthew 19:3–9), my prayer is that we'll experience healing, conviction, or both, depending on what the Holy Spirit determines we need. Let us come with open hearts.

In first-century Judaism it was nearly impossible for a formerly married woman to remain unmarried, for both economic and social reasons.[44] And it was mostly the men who got to decide whether they wanted a divorce, not the women. There were two prominent rabbinic schools of thought on divorce (one conservative, hardly any reason for divorce; one liberal, divorce as you please). The laxer one meant a man could divorce his wife for just about any selfish reason, thus leaving her destitute, so long as he did it "Moses's way" with a written certificate.

This is where Jesus looked the men in the eye and said, *Excuse me, but might I have a word?*

Jesus confronted the religious leaders (and others) who were coming to the Torah looking for loopholes on divorce rather than paying attention to why Moses had come up with the provision of a divorce certificate in the first place. It wasn't so husbands could dispose of their wives when their wives didn't bear them enough sons or had lost their touch in the kitchen with the chicken potpie. It was because people's hearts had become hard (Matt. 19:8). They had stopped marveling at the wonder of God creating male and female and joining them together to become one flesh, a union that was not to be broken. They'd turned marriage into a self-serving arrangement when it was supposed to be a permanent covenant of loving commitment that reflected God's own steadfast heart toward His people.

Once again, Jesus had no interest in what religious boxes could legally be checked but what heart issues were at stake. He was concerned about the injustices toward women who could not easily take care of themselves if abandoned by their husbands. He was intent on shoring up everyone's perspective, both men's and women's, on marriage and its sacredness before God. Only in the case of adultery, Jesus says, is divorce permitted. (Many scholars would argue Jesus's intent covers other serious covenant-breaking actions, such as abandonment, as mentioned by Paul in 1 Cor. 7:15.)

Paul later teaches that marriage between a man and woman is a reflection of the union of Christ and His church. He is our bridegroom and we are His bride. In singleness, His sufficiency sustains, which I can testify to firsthand. In both good and hard marriages, His goodness and glory are revealed. For those who have suffered through a divorce, Christ is the mender of wounded hearts and the restorer of broken lives. No matter what your status—married, divorced, remarried, separated, single—Jesus's heart is positioned toward you.

John Stott said it so beautifully when he observed, "The Pharisees were preoccupied with the grounds for divorce; Jesus with the institution of marriage."[45] How much Jesus wants us to understand His good will for our lives. The life of a believer isn't about checking legal boxes so we can be released from what we're tired of. It's truly about discovering, again and again, His heart behind His good ways.

DAY 28

TELL THE TRUTH

"Again, you have heard that it was said to our ancestors, You must not break your oath, but you must keep your oaths to the Lord. But I tell you, don't take an oath at all: either by heaven, because it is God's throne; or by the earth, because it is his footstool; or by Jerusalem, because it is the city of the great King. Do not swear by your head, because you cannot make a single hair white or black. But let your 'yes' mean 'yes,' and your 'no' mean 'no.' Anything more than this is from the evil one."

Matthew 5:33–37

THIS IS THE FOURTH OF the six *you've heard it saids* where Jesus reaches into the cupboard of Old Testament law, pulls out something familiar to everyone as if it were a jar of honey or a can of tomatoes, cracks open the lid, and tells us how it was *truly* meant to be used. We don't think too much about oath taking today unless we're watching a movie and someone ends up on the witness stand. But in ancient Israel, taking oaths was a common practice. People swore they were going to do this or that, and if they swore by the Lord's name, or something close, it was considered binding.

As with everything else Jesus addressed in this section of His Sermon, people were missing God's heart behind His commands. In this case they were tinkering with the oath itself to get around its intended purpose which was to ensure a person followed through on his or her commitment. The clever religious leaders came up with things like, *When I said I'd pay you back, I didn't swear by God but by Jerusalem, which isn't as binding, so don't count on it. Or, If you see me worshipping in the temple without remorse for my wrongdoing, it's because I didn't technically break my oath.* The whole thing had gotten so ridiculous, and Jesus was calling it out. He reminded them that even swearing by "lesser" things like heaven, earth, Jerusalem, or by one's own head were all things that belonged to God anyhow.

To make it simple, Jesus just told His disciples to stop taking oaths. When you say yes, follow through, and when you say no, mean it. Honesty shouldn't require an elaborate vow.

I wish I could say that we as the people of God have grown out of tinkering with our promises and commitments. But we still parse them when we want out of them: *Did I actually sign on the dotted line that I would do that?* We make excuses about why we can't make an engagement, when in reality, a better offer popped up: *I'll just let them know I'm not feeling well.* We try to wiggle out of our *yeses* and *noes*, amending what we've promised while trying to come off as honest. This is to say nothing about flat out lying to people.

The upside to all this is that Jesus provides a more honest, straightforward way of interacting with one another. Instead of finagling with the letter of the law to accommodate our dishonest hearts, Jesus redeems our hearts so our commitments and promises will be ones we naturally want to keep. Oaths won't be necessary. (This doesn't mean that oaths should never be taken. That would be to bend Jesus's message in the opposite direction of error. The point is that oaths had been abused, and dishonesty in the human heart is what made them necessary in the first place.)

The premium Jesus places on honesty and integrity is liberating to our relationships and proves He wants the best for them. Can you imagine living in a world where you never had to guess a person's motives or whether they would actually stay true to their word? So many of life's heartaches would vanish, not to mention the paperwork and legal bills. How wonderful not to have to read between the lines to figure out what a friend actually meant, to be able to depend on a family member's commitment. How lovely to be dependable ourselves. Imagine living within the security of such trustworthy relationships?

Is there an unkept commitment you can still fulfill? A promise to someone you can make good on? Maybe it's something as simple as showing up because you said you would. Or being appropriately transparent for why you need to change your plans instead of shading your real reason with a row of emojis. How refreshing is a trustworthy yes or no, a simple word that can be counted on.

DAY 29

GOING BEYOND GETTING EVEN

"You have heard that it was said, 'An eye for an eye and a tooth for a tooth.' But I tell you, don't resist an evildoer. On the contrary, if anyone slaps you on your right cheek, turn the other to him also. As for the one who wants to sue you and take away your shirt, let him have your coat as well. And if anyone forces you to go one mile, go with him two. Give to the one who asks you, and don't turn away from the one who wants to borrow from you."

Matthew 5:38–42

I IMAGINE THERE'S SOMEONE IN your life who has deeply hurt you. Perhaps you can't bear the thought of them getting anything less than their just deserts. At the very least you need them to be sorry and to grovel; a bit of their blood wouldn't hurt. Showing them mercy, offering them a gift they don't deserve, hanging in there with them an extra foot, much less a mile, feels reckless and preposterous not to mention just plain impossible. Surely Jesus can't really mean we're to respond to those who have hurt us with love instead of retaliation.

"An eye for an eye and a tooth for a tooth" is a phrase we still use today, and it refers to repaying an offender in equal measurement to the offense (*lex talionis*). In the Old Testament it also ensured a punishment didn't exceed its corresponding offense. You wouldn't put a child in jail for stealing a piece of bread, for example. This commandment "had the double effect of defining justice and restraining revenge."[46] Most of us who have been wounded by someone can get behind the original application of this law because it means the person who hurt us will get what's coming to them. It makes life reasonably "fair."

But Jesus redefines this Old Testament law in a nearly inconceivable way. He reveals that grace, love, mercy, and forgiveness are more powerful and redemptive responses than getting even. Where Moses's law took the stance of "show no pity" in matters of injustice, Jesus's redefinition of this old command was closer to "always show mercy."[47]

John Stott says about this passage, "Nowhere is the challenge of the Sermon greater. Nowhere is the distinctness of the Christian counter-culture more obvious."[48] I think we can all wholeheartedly agree, which is why I'm thankful he also wrote, "Nowhere is our need of the power of the Holy Spirit (whose first fruit is love) more compelling."[49] We cannot muster up otherworldly, Christlike love toward those who have hurt us without the power of His Spirit transforming our hearts. And we cannot do it without first remembering that Christ died for us while we were *yet sinners* (Rom. 5:8). We can only show the forgiveness we've been shown.

Christians throughout the centuries have debated how "far" Jesus's words are meant to be taken. Does He mean there can be no military, no punishment for lawbreaking citizens, no recompence for injustice? These are reasonable discussions, but for most of us the question is simply: What are we doing with Jesus's words when it comes to the person who hurt us, who walked out on us when were young, who slandered us in some public arena, who chose another best friend? What does obedience to Jesus look like in *those* places?

Only the Holy Spirit can show you what love looks like in the face of wounding. What you can know for sure is that it will not look like paying someone back wrong for wrong, bearing the burden of revenge while ravaged with a desire for the downfall of the one who hurt you. The apostle Peter tells us that when we suffer for doing good, we can entrust ourselves to our faithful Creator (1 Pet. 4:19). When we love instead of retaliate, we place ourselves in His care, handing over to Him the heavy responsibility of carrying out justice with the possibility of bringing about restoration.

What Jesus is asking of you will resemble the unexpected. Instead of reacting with the same harshness or aloofness shown you, a gift of grace or an act of mercy will be the new currency with which you will settle accounts.

Heavenly Father, I acknowledge that You did not give me what I deserved, but instead You loved me while I was in my sin. I need You to help me show love to the one who has wounded me. I can't do it without the outpouring of Your Spirit.

DAY 30

LOVE YOUR ENEMIES

"You have heard that it was said, 'Love your neighbor' and hate your enemy. But I tell you, love your enemies and pray for those who persecute you, so that you may be children of your Father in heaven. For he causes his sun to rise on the evil and the good, and sends rain on the righteous and the unrighteous. For if you love those who love you, what reward will you have? Don't even the tax collectors do the same? And if you greet only your brothers and sisters, what are you doing out of the ordinary? Don't even the Gentiles do the same?"

Matthew 5:43–47

Remember the "greater righteousness" Jesus talked about earlier in His Sermon, the kind that exceeds that of the Pharisees? Here He's putting the final touches on what that righteousness looks like in our everyday lives with perhaps its most climactic expression yet: love your enemies.

Jesus quotes the last of the six *you have heard it saids*, this time with a twist. The Old Testament law did indeed command God's people to love their neighbors, but nowhere did the law say Israel was to hate her enemies. It appears this was just the commonsense conclusion everyone had come to.

Jesus confronts their misunderstanding with some common sense of His own, the kind of logic that's based on how our heavenly Father treats us, not on how we typically treat one another. Jesus points out that both good and evil people pull back the curtains in the morning and are warmly greeted by sunlight. The crops that belong to the nice farmers and the not-so-nice ones benefit from the heat and energy of that same sun. Friendly neighbors as well as irritating troublemakers enjoy spring showers that fill up pitchers, water grass and gardens, and keep harvest fields drinking. In other words, if God showers these necessary gifts on the good and the bad, the deserving and the super annoying, shouldn't we also shower love on our enemies, a force more powerful than sunshine and rain?

Jesus continues, because apparently we're not uncomfortable enough yet. He gives examples of two groups of people the Jews would have really frowned upon—tax collectors and Gentiles. According to the Jewish mindset, these were the pagans at the bottom of the barrel. Surprisingly, Jesus upholds them as people who show love to one another and greet their own warmly. His point was that His followers shouldn't be high-fiving one another for being kind to people who are kind to them. Pretty much everyone does that, even the Gentiles with their myriad false gods and the tax collectors who take their countrymen's money on behalf of Rome. That kind of "love" doesn't set God's people apart. It's not extraordinary, and it's not the stuff of "greater righteousness."

If we want to follow Jesus, we must deeply love not only our neighbors, friends, and family, but our enemies too. We must pray for those who come against us. This will testify to the reality that we're children of the Father because this is His nature. Dietrich Bonhoeffer wrote, "The love for our enemies takes us along the way of the cross and into fellowship with the Crucified. The more we are driven along this road, the more certain is the victory of love over the enemy's hatred."[50]

I don't know what enemy Jesus is calling you to love and pray for, but I do know it's a matter of fellowship with the crucified Christ. When you love those who have hurt you, you are literally, as Paul wrote to the Philippians, fellowshipping with Him in His sufferings. A certain communion with Jesus can only happen at the table of unjust suffering. When you love and pray for your enemy, you're pulling up a chair at His table, intimately getting to know the ultimate Suffering Servant. Loving your enemy is a three-person affair. We can't do it without Jesus, and when we do it with Him, we find Him an even deeper, closer, nearer friend.

Make today the day you trade bitterness, anger, and revenge for love, kindness, and intercessory prayer. Draw close to your Savior who suffered on behalf of His enemies. In so doing, you will both bear and reflect the good and gracious nature of your Father in heaven.

DAY 31

BEING WHOLE

"Be perfect, therefore, as your heavenly Father is perfect."

Matthew 5:48

One of the most majestic parts of the Amazon River is where it all begins—the famous "Meeting of the Waters." Here, the Solimoes and Negro tributaries join to form what the Brazilians consider the official start of the Amazon. What makes this landmark so distinct is the visible disparity between the two rivers. The camel colored Solimoes and the darkly tinted Negro merge at different speeds, different temperatures, and are made up of different sediments. They eventually blend but not before miles of stubborn resistance. For me, it is always a visible reminder of what it means to belong to Christ (justification) and the day-by-day process of looking more like Him (sanctification).

You may remember that in Matthew 5:17 Jesus began a section of His Sermon on what true righteousness in His kingdom looks like in our everyday lives. Today He sums up that portion with a call to perfection, as our heavenly Father is perfect. (*Phew,* we all exclaim, because *this sounds easy.*) If anyone else has ever been disheartened by the word *perfect* here, now is a good time to learn that its Greek translation *teleios* is "not moral perfection but having wholehearted orientation toward God."[51] Words such as *whole*, *complete*, or *virtuous*,[52] get us closer to its meaning. Instead of trying to perfectly meet a moral standard so we can earn God's favor, we are instead summoned to be undivided, wholly like Him. We need no longer live as a river split down the middle, torn between our desire for righteousness and our longing to live at our own speed, colored by sin's propensities.

I remember, especially in my younger years, attempting to curb my affections and heal the desires of my heart by trying to outwardly do the right things out of my own reservoir of strength. It about put me on the edge of a breakdown. Have you ever felt this way? Like whoever you're trying to be on the outside is so far from who you know yourself to be on the inside that the effort to align the two becomes overwhelming, even oppressive?

If so, do you hear the hope in Jesus's words? His call to *teleios* meets us in our disparity and incongruence. It makes it possible for our hearts and actions to run in tandem, and ultimately resemble His image. It puts forth the reality that we can be whole, virtuous people, "not one thing on the outside but another on the inside."[53] This good news is consistent with what we've reflected on the past few days: Jesus isn't only concerned with outward behaviors like murder, adultery, divorce, dishonesty, and revenge, but also what is brewing inside our hearts such as anger, lust, trickery, hate, and imagining ways to skirt commitment. Jesus desires for us to be complete people who not only belong to Him but look like Him.

This will require grace, of course. Not only grace that saves us from our sin and is waiting to restore us when we fall short of His righteousness, but grace that empowers us to live the life Jesus says we can. It's grace that's at work in our hearts to help us become wholly righteous. It makes possible *teleios* as a way of life, no longer fractured between who we know we are and who we want to be.

But we must participate with God's grace to be whole and holy. "Grace is not opposed to effort, it is opposed to earning,"[54] said Dallas Willard. It is true we cannot accomplish this by going full-throttle Pharisee to achieve perfection, but we also can't just sit back doing nothing because, *grace*. Jesus hasn't backed His standards down. World Cup holiness is still the arena He wants us to play ball in, because He's made whole-person righteousness available to us. This kind of purity toward God, this continuity between your inner and outer life is possible for you now!

Oh, what a glorious call *teleios* is. In Christ, undivided affection for the Lord that inhabits your heart and guides your actions is possible. What an uplifting reality for those weary of performing while your heart desperately needs tending and renewal. What a joy to flow at His speed, be immersed into His righteousness and absorbed by His likeness.

DAY 32

GIVING FOR THE RIGHT REASONS

"Be careful not to practice your righteousness in front of others to be seen by them. Otherwise, you have no reward with your Father in heaven. So whenever you give to the poor, don't sound a trumpet before you, as the hypocrites do in the synagogues and on the streets, to be applauded by people. Truly I tell you, they have their reward. But when you give to the poor, don't let your left hand know what your right hand is doing, so that your giving may be in secret. And your Father who sees in secret will reward you."

Matthew 6:1–4

As we closed Matthew 5, we realized that sinful dispositions are at the root of sinful actions. But as we open Matthew 6, a question is naturally raised: What about righteous-looking actions? Can sinful dispositions be behind those, too? This is where Jesus goes next, and the continuity in His teaching is evident: sinful hearts give way to sinful actions, but they can also be the motivation for our best-looking deeds. Once again, Jesus's teaching on whole-person righteousness doesn't leave any part of us alone.

For example, you may be at a point in your Christian life where you're not routinely angry, you tell the truth to others, you have integrity at work, and you don't let your mind revel in thoughts that might one day lead to an affair. Yet when you give, pray, and fast, you need people to take note of your sacrifice and all-around godly fabulousness. Jesus teaches that this is a problem. When our actions on the outside look good but we're motivated by the applause of others, we need His restoration to come home to our hearts.

In ancient Judaism, giving to the poor was standard practice. Notice Jesus didn't say *if* you give but *when* you give. Yet He didn't want His followers to give like the hypocrites who blew their trumpets so people would be alerted to applaud. (He didn't want them to, as we like to say, "toot their own horn.") Today we don't make a habit of blowing trumpets while dropping our tithe in the offering plate, but we are not without our modern-day instruments. We have social media and the Internet and all manner of ways to sound our horns of generosity and service. Our desire to be applauded and noticed is so seductive that Jesus said to give so secretly that your left hand won't even know what your right hand is doing. This ensures you're giving for the right reasons—to honor God and bless others.

"But wait," you may wondering, "why did Jesus tell us to do *visible* acts of goodness that shine like lights in Matthew 5:16, only to turn around and tell us to do *invisible*, secret good deeds in Matthew 6:1?" If we look closely, we see that it's all about where we want the glory to go. If we love others tangibly and visibly, we do it so that God will be glorified. And when we give secretly, we glorify Him by believing His approval and reward are more important than anyone else's.

Much of Jesus's teaching here gets down to reward. If the reward you're after is a pat on the back, more social media followers, or invitations to important parties, those are exactly the rewards you'll get. The problem is that these accolades do nothing to grant us self-worth and only leave us hungering for more. How often we sacrifice the Father's reward for a handful of human accolades that taste so good we need a whole bag of them the next time. It's a merciless existence of giving for the sake of getting, except the getting never satisfies.

I understand this at my core. My outward behaviors are not my biggest problem presently; rather God is dealing with my desire for the people closest to me to see how generous and sacrificial I've been. If my generosity isn't noticed, will I still be worth something to them? You can see what a disastrous cycle this is, one from which Jesus set us free when He said, "And your Father who sees in secret will reward you."

Let these words settle into your heart.

Giving and serving in obscurity is never hidden from our Father's view. He doesn't miss a gift given or a penny bestowed. He sees beyond what humans can see—not just what is righteous looking but also what is righteous in essence. And what our Father sees, He rewards. The simple and obvious takeaway is that there's no comparison between a person's applause and God's reward.

Dear friend, in Christ we have the power not only to live quietly generous lives but to set our earthly trumpets aside. For a heavenly trumpet is coming, and on that day, in the place of human praise, we will hear the only voice that matters saying, "Well done, my good and faithful servant."

DAY 33

PRAYING LIKE GOD'S BELOVED CHILDREN

"Whenever you pray, you must not be like the hypocrites, because they love to pray standing in the synagogues and on the street corners to be seen by people. Truly I tell you, they have their reward. But when you pray, go into your private room, shut your door, and pray to your Father who is in secret. And your Father who sees in secret will reward you. When you pray, don't babble like the Gentiles, since they imagine they'll be heard for their many words. Don't be like them, because your Father knows the things you need before you ask him."

Matthew 6:5–8

Sometimes knowing what *not* to do is as helpful as knowing what to do. This approach helps me particularly in the kitchen. Whenever I make gingersnaps, I can hear my mom telling me not to overbake them. My brother reminds me not to overproof my bread dough. Every cook I've ever met says don't skimp on the salt. Jesus takes this approach when it comes to His teaching on prayer. Before telling us how we should pray, He tells us how *not* to pray.

He first points to two groups of people His followers were not to pray like—the hypocrites and the Gentiles, each for a different reason. The religious hypocrites recited prayers in prominent places to be noticed and esteemed by people, and the pagan Gentiles carried on with a string of mindless words in hopes of manipulating their unpredictable, faraway gods. It was customary for the Jewish people to pray three times a day. But some of them arranged to be at conspicuous locations such as the synagogues and busy street corners during the hour of prayer so people could see how godly they were. These were the ones Jesus referred to as *hypocrites.* Because when you have to display how godly you are, there's a good chance you're not.

Jesus invites us to step out of the exhausting comparison limelight and into our quiet places, the ones hidden from our friends and neighbors so we're not tempted to exchange rich communion with our Father for the reward of people thinking we're pretty great. Much the way God sees our secret generosity, He sees our secret praying. But Jesus adds the interesting detail that our Father not only sees what we do in the secret place, He *Himself* is also "in secret." Some aspect of His being is uniquely present with us when we seek Him in prayer in those hidden spaces. He inhabits our secret place.

I believe the reverse is also true. In our modern day where praying publicly three times a day is not the norm, we may be too embarrassed to ask a hurting neighbor or coworker if we can pray for them. We may be afraid to pray publicly before a meal in the name of Jesus. Whether it's praying for the applause of people or not praying because of what people might think, both reveal that the opinions of others have greater influence over our prayer life than the opinion of God. May we confess this in our secret spaces so we can also be bold pray-ers in our public places.

Different from the religious hypocrites who prayed to the one, true God, the Gentiles prayed to numerous gods they believed governed things like the sun, the rain, and their crops. But their gods were capricious. From day to day, the Gentiles could only hope their gods had gotten up on the right side of the bed and that their repetitious babbling would convince them into giving the Gentiles what they needed. Against this kind of praying, Jesus says, *Rest. Your heavenly Father isn't caught off guard by your sudden job loss, your struggles in marriage, the college tuition that's due, the aching in your heart for a companion, the medical diagnosis.* He knows what you need before you can even get the words out. He doesn't have to be persuaded to hear or to care. You get to pray differently from the pagans because your God is different!

What an invitation is before you today to commune with your loving heavenly Father. He sees you in your secret place of praying. He knows what you need before you even pour your heart out to Him. He isn't impressed by elaborate displays of piety. He only desires real relationship with you. And He is nothing like the distant and uniformed gods of the pagans; rather He is all-knowing, loving, and present.

Before you begin the rest of the day's tasks and activities, spend some time in prayer in your secret place. He promises His presence and reward.

DAY 34

PRAY LIKE THIS

"Therefore, you should pray like this: 'Our Father in heaven, your name be honored as holy. Your kingdom come. Your will be done on earth as it is in heaven.'"

Matthew 6:9–10

Praying feels like one of those things we should just know how to do, like talking and conversing. We have this longing in our souls to commune with the One who made us, who knows us better than we know ourselves. Yet prayer is one of the hardest disciplines for most Christians I know. Perhaps it should make us all feel better that Jesus's beloved disciple John asked Jesus to *teach* him and the other disciples how to pray (Luke 11:1). This tells me that John and his friends needed some instruction, and so do we.

Jesus responded to John with a model prayer we often refer to as *the Lord's Prayer*. Some prefer to call it *the Disciples' Prayer* since we're the ones who pray it.

One of the first things we notice is that it begins with God. This might seem fairly obvious, but, let's face it, we don't always start here. Most of our praying begins with *us*. My home is currently under construction, and every morning I have to discipline myself not to start with "Lord, please let the workers show up today. If I don't get my house back soon, I'm going to . . . ," and then I think of something really dramatic to say.

In much more desperate times, I've begun with how scared I am, how hurt, or how lonely. This might be a good time to say that I don't think there's anything unholy about bringing our raw hearts and emotions straight to the Lord without first going through a series of formalities. This is earnest fellowship. But there's a foundation to our prayers that all our requests and petitions must be laid upon, and that is the praise of His name and the desire that His rule and reign come about in all things.

When we begin by lifting high His name, we acknowledge that no one's fame or glory is more important than His, especially our own. And by placing His renown in front of all others, we testify to His inestimable worth. Prayers that begin here set our hearts at ease, whether we're troubled by swarming fears without or anxieties simmering within because no one and no thing is more powerful, more good, more present, more glorious than our heavenly Father. So we say with confidence and delight, "Hallowed be *Your* name."

In enthusiastic tandem with this declaration, we can't help but also pray for His rule of justice, righteousness, peace, and love to come to bear on the ruined parts of our world and for His desires and aims to be accomplished here on earth just the way they are working all things out in heaven. And when we find we aren't longing for these things, it's usually because our pride and personal agendas are at odds with God's will and renown. We only find this out when we pray the way Jesus tells us to.

The Lord's Prayer makes certain that before we get to any of our personal petitions we have the privilege of correcting course, bending our wills toward His despite our resistance, clinging to our Father's ways even when leaving behind our own feels like it just might kill us. Here, at the top of our prayers, we place ourselves under the rule and reign of our loving heavenly Father. Here we align our hearts and ambitions with His! Here we say, *Your name* above our ego, our being right, our being esteemed by others. Here we declare *Your ways* above all others because no one is greater, more loving, more worthy than the Father in heaven who is *ours.*

When we start with Him, all other petitions are sure to fall in holy line.

Heavenly Father, before getting to our many sincere and pressing prayer requests today, we begin by praying that Your name be honored. We long for You to bring our chaos under Your rule and for Your will to be achieved above our own.

DAY 35

OUR DAILY BREAD

"Give us today our daily bread."

Matthew 6:11

In our modern day, the word *bread* brings many images to mind. Crusty boules lining the shelves of a local bakery, the welcoming aroma of fresh loaves rising, the entire point of any sandwich. But for the Jews listening to Jesus's words, *bread* stood less for carbs and comfort and more for daily sustenance. Bread was a symbol, said Martin Luther, for "everything necessary for the preservation of this life."[55] Consider the gamut we cover in our prayers, from the lofty places of desiring God's reign and renown to seeking Him for our most basic needs. Our heavenly Father cares about it all because He cares about us.

The idea of bread would have also evoked rich cultural memories special to God's people, such as God providing manna to Israel in the wilderness. Six days a week the people gathered what God had provided, and never did they lack. For Jesus's first-century listeners the precedent had been set—asking God for bread meant expecting He would provide. How much more is this true for us today as Jesus would just a bit later describe Himself as the bread of life?

God's storehouses are stocked with everything you need for life and fullness in Christ—provision for your daily, physical needs and for your soul a rich supply of peace, hope, and joy.

This asking God to meet our daily and fundamental needs postures us in a position of dependency and expectation. In our Western culture where we are leading the charge in number of storage units, many have more provision than we know what to do with. Dependence on our Father for daily necessities can seem a foreign idea. This is not true, however, for much of the world. Many move throughout their day unsure of where their next meal will come from.

I'm privileged to know orphans and vulnerable children from the Eastern European country of Moldova. One in particular recalls spending the night in a field as a little boy when in between homes. He knows what it means to cry out to God for daily bread. In the Amazon I've talked with countless jungle pastors who, in the middle of crop-destroying floods, have had to claw their way to the tops of trees for a piece of fruit for their family. *Give us our daily bread* is a familiar and communal cry of Christ's body throughout the world.

As numerous as the cries are the stories of God's timely and often miraculous provision. Families in the Amazon have testified of fish leaping into their canoes, *without a fishing pole*, in the middle of famine conditions. Moldovan orphans tell stories of praying to God from sparse bedrooms in abusive homes who were soon delivered into JMI's loving transitional living homes. When we seek God to meet our needs, we find Him to be a powerful Provider and also a kind Father. Just think how the image of "Father" shows loving intimacy for His children as well as sovereign power.[56] Deep, daily dependence on Him yields His provision, but, what is more, it yields His presence.

You may have noticed that the first part of the Lord's Prayer is oriented around God while the second half focuses on human needs and relationships. We begin praying an assortment of *Your's* and then move on to many heartfelt and pressing *our's*. That our heavenly Father bids us bring our needs and desires before Him stands in stark comparison to the Gentiles who in their desperation could only plead with their fickle and uninformed gods.

Seek Him, dear one, for your daily bread. He is eager to meet your needs.

DAY 36

FORGIVE US AS WE FORGIVE

"And forgive us our debts, as we also have forgiven our debtors. . . . For if you forgive others their offenses, your heavenly Father will forgive you as well. But if you don't forgive others, your Father will not forgive your offenses."

Mathew 6:12, 14–15

The Lord's Prayer is economic when you think about it. Had I been the one who asked Jesus to *teach us to pray*, I would have expected Him to respond with something much longer, more thorough and detailed. But in a sense Jesus covers just about everything by covering just a few things. He sounds the major chords of our lives, which naturally include the individual notes of our more specific longings. What needs or desires do we have that aren't somehow accounted for under the sweeping crescendos of worship, food and shelter, forgiveness and reconciled relationships, freedom from evil?

If you're like me, though, you might not have thought to assign forgiveness such a starring role in the prayer. Aligning with God's will and ways? We get that part. Bread, we wholeheartedly are on board with. We can also get behind the strong argument for needing God's forgiveness. But must He have added the part about *our* needing to forgive the debtors in our lives—those who owe us? Why the extra explanation about how inextricably connected forgiving others is to God's forgiving us? I think John Stott addresses this beautifully. "Forgiveness," he says "is as indispensable to the life and health of the soul as food is for the body."[57]

Indispensable, he says. Jesus accentuates our need to be forgiven and to forgive others because without it flowing in and out of our beings, life in the kingdom is impossible.

A few months ago I flew back to Northern Virginia to attend my mom and dad's last Sunday at Reston Bible Church, the church they founded nearly fifty years ago. I saw people I have known since birth—former youth group leaders and Sunday school teachers, the parents of some of my best childhood friends, missionaries, and longtime servants in the local body. It was an emotional ride through decades of memories; my mascara was all but gone before I found my seat. Peering around the sanctuary that morning, spotting faces old and young, some with unfathomable stories, I'll tell you this: the church wouldn't have made it to its first anniversary—much less it's fiftieth—without the regular practice of forgiveness. It's what greases the wheels so we as the church can keep riding together with the top down. Without it, relationships come to a grinding halt.

Sometimes forgiveness feels perfectly impossible, though, and I understand this. Whether we've been deeply wounded by a fellow Christ follower or an unbeliever, offering forgiveness is enormously challenging—especially when the offender is not the least bit sorry or contrite. That always just burns me up. And how can we possibly do what Jesus tells us to do later in Matthew's Gospel: forgive from our *hearts* (Matt. 18:35)?

When we're caught in that place of "impossible forgiveness," it helps to remember what we've already learned in Jesus's Sermon: reconciled and harmonious relationships are deeply important to Him. Forgiveness makes this possible. It restores wellness to afflicted relationships, and if the offending party isn't sorry or reconciliation isn't possible, it restores wellness to *us*. We can't indefinitely survive caught in the briar patch of unforgiveness, interminably pricked by bitterness and tangled in revenge. It's a slow, dark dying.

So, here, Jesus gives us the liberating gift of forgiveness, both giving it and receiving it. Like breathing in and out, we can't do one without the other. God's forgiving us is predicated on our forgiving others and vice versa. At first this seems to pose a problem for our theological foundation of "saved by grace," yet when we've experienced the profound, undeserved forgiveness of God, solely by grace, extending it to others becomes the necessary outflow of our hearts. I would also contend this works in reverse—forgiving others acquaints us with its price, its value, its power, its gift. We cannot help but know Jesus's forgiveness for ourselves when we're in the middle of depending on His grace to forgive others.

What do you need God's forgiveness for? Whom do you need to forgive? The riches in Christ Jesus are able to supply its coming and going. Ask Him today to help you forgive from your heart. It's a prayer Jesus taught us to pray, and whatever He tells us to ask for, He promises to provide.

DAY 37

LET US NOT BE OVERWHELMED BY EVIL

"And do not bring us into temptation, but deliver us from the evil one."

Matthew 6:13

I DISCOVERED UPON WRITING TODAY'S devotion that in some ways I least connect with this part of the Lord's Prayer. I think it's the word "evil" that's caused me to mentally skip over it as though I were a kid trying to avoid a dastardly crack in the sidewalk. Maybe the idea of evil feels a bit dramatic, a little too over-the-top for my morning prayers. Does Satan have to be crouching behind every bush? I think we can sometimes identify more with *deliver us from a Target shopping addiction, an extra cocktail in the evening, or sharing morsels of gossip at work*, but *evil* can feel extreme.

Until, of course, we come face-to-face with it and are jolted into acknowledging the presence of evil in our world, in our hearts. You may be facing the consequences of someone else's addiction, hatred, sexual abuse, violence, immorality, or injustice. Whether you're right in the middle of the fight of your life or "evil" and "temptation" feel a little sensational at the moment, we are all in desperate need of being spared from sinful enticement and delivered from darkness. I may wish evil were something I could sweep under the carpet, but Peter tells us the source of evil, the enemy himself, is in fact pacing on top of the carpet, like a roaring lion looking for those he can devour (1 Pet. 5:8). I need to get Jesus's strong language back into my prayer rotation.

There are two parts to today's petition, so let's begin with the first one: temptation. Jesus tells us to pray that God will not bring us into temptation. We know from James 1:13 that God doesn't tempt us to sin. We also know from Paul that God always makes a way of escape whenever we're tempted (1 Cor. 10:13). The disciples listening to Jesus would have known that God purifies His people by testing them through trials (think the wilderness and Deut. 8). The difference here is that God's testing is always for our good whereas the enemy's tempting is for our downfall.[58] Praying that we not be led into temptation seems to be a plea for God not to allow temptation to be so overwhelming that we give into it and then find ourselves a slave to the evil one's agenda. This "request is about preservation from sin in temptation."[59]

Do you need the Lord to preserve you during an intense season of temptation? Are you suffering from the effects of evil inflicted upon you? As you pray for God to preserve you, ask Him to also deliver you from what is dark and wicked. This is the second part of the petition. Sometimes our trials can be so heavy, our suffering so long, the boughs of our resolve begin to bend, and we feel that snapping under temptation's weight is inevitable. Jesus's beloved disciple John would later remind us in this instance that the One who is in us is greater than the one who is in the world (1 John 4:4).

So we pray, *Lord, don't allow life's burdens to be so heavy I give in to sin. Don't let temptation be so great it overwhelms me. Instead, rescue me from evil and the evil one. For the power of darkness cannot begin to overcome the light You've placed within me. Help me participate with You in avoiding temptation whenever I can. And when it springs on me without notice, hold me fast from sin, and ultimately deliver me from Satan's evil agenda in this world.*

We know as believers that we will traverse valleys of suffering and that temptation will whisper our names in our most vulnerable moments. As we contend against the alluring pull of sin by fleeing from it and as we seek God's rescue by praying for it, what desires to overthrow us can be the thing that refines us. So let us pray the prayer Jesus taught us to pray, and after having braved the world, the flesh, and the devil, we will emerge not devoured but delivered.

DAY 38

FASTING NOT FOR APPLAUSE

"Whenever you fast, don't be gloomy like the hypocrites. For they disfigure their faces so that their fasting is obvious to people. Truly I tell you, they have their reward. But when you fast, put oil on your head and wash your face, so that your fasting isn't obvious to others but to your Father who is in secret. And your Father who sees in secret will reward you."

Matthew 6:16–18

There is only one answer for why the scent of bread baking in the oven happens to be wafting through my home on the same day I am writing about fasting: I am a horrible planner. It has followed me through several rooms reminding me why fasting is such a challenge. If things like forgiveness and loving one's enemy go against our emotional inclinations, fasting goes against our physical ones. God's creative and elaborate gift of food is not only immensely enjoyable; it also nourishes our bodies so we can think, exercise, grow, and not be angry at every living soul who walks into the room. We come by the term *hangry* earnestly.

Fasting was something the Jewish people in Jesus's day practiced regularly. It was part of their routine. Notice once again that Jesus doesn't say *if* you fast but *when* you fast. In the Old Testament, Israel fasted for numerous reasons—when they were mourning, repenting, confessing sin, interceding for others, or simply desperate for help. As one of my friends put it, "People fasted when they were overwhelmed."

That Jesus's original audience was fasting wasn't the problem; *why* they were fasting was the concern. Like the practices of giving to the poor and praying regularly, fasting had become another way to garner pats on the back. When the religious people fasted, they wanted to make sure they looked the part—a scant sickly, a touch gaunt. You know how this goes—if we're going to sacrifice for righteousness's sake, we should at a bare minimum accentuate our efforts so people can take note. *My, how devoted to God you must be, skipping the pancakes as you are. I can hardly think of a holier soul.*

Jesus in turn suggested we do the opposite. We should throw onlookers off the trail—put on our makeup, do our hair, emote, so people won't know we haven't eaten. This way we can be assured our hearts are in the right place, that we're fasting as a way of seeking God and affirming that His reward is better than a person's accolade. It's that "greater righteousness" Jesus is so concerned about, remember? The one that exceeds that of the scribes and Pharisees and has to do with both action and heart.

The problem today is that most of us aren't worrying about people applauding us for fasting because we're not fasting at all. (We sure took care of that temptation, didn't we?) It's true the New Testament doesn't talk about fasting nearly as often as the Old, but it's an important practice for us as Christ followers. When we fast, we forgo something natural (the baking bread) in pursuit of the supernatural (the Bread of Life). We set our hopes on what's to come when Christ returns, specifically the wedding supper of the Lamb. Fasting conditions us to say *no* to ourselves and *yes* to God. It teaches us contentment and joy when our physical hunger isn't being satisfied. When we're lacking food's nourishment, we feast on God's presence. Fasting takes the focus off ourselves and places it onto God and others. Fasting is prayer's powerful companion, the habit we add when what we're seeking is impossible.

So perhaps Jesus's command that we fast for the right reasons is also a needed reminder that we fast in the first place.

Consider setting aside a meal or going without food from sunup to sundown, assuming this is a medically feasible practice for you. Fast from food for the purpose of feasting on what God has prepared for you. As your stomach pangs for your morning oatmeal or afternoon turkey sandwich, let it be a reminder of how your soul pants for the presence of the living God. And when you fast, don't forget to sharpen the knot in your tie or add a touch of gloss to your lips—no one needs to know you were praying instead of eating during the lunch hour except your Father in heaven who promises to reward you.

Heavenly Father, give us the grace to occasionally set aside our daily bread so we can experience the nourishing goodness of the Bread of Life. And may we find that spending time with You is our greatest reward.

DAY 39

WHERE TO STORE YOUR TREASURE

"Don't store up for yourselves treasures on earth, where moth and rust destroy and where thieves break in and steal. But store up for yourselves treasures in heaven, where neither moth nor rust destroys, and where thieves don't break in and steal. For where your treasure is, there your heart will be also."

Matthew 6:19–21

I don't know any Christ follower who hasn't had some knock-down-drag-out moments with the Lord over this passage. We Americans find much joy in our possessions. We love them so, our new pieces of furniture, vehicles, tech gadgets, clothing, vacation homes, coffee makers. And yet Jesus is pragmatic about the stuff we set our affections on—they're temporary, fleeting, eroding. In our anxiousness to keep accumulating, we may think, *Oh, but we have mothballs now and chemicals that prevent rust and nifty cameras that keep thieves away. Jesus, we've solved this problem!*

But of course we know that today's treasures fade just in different ways. Those jeans that were cropped perfectly last year are ridiculous looking now. The television that couldn't possibly cast a sharper picture, eighteen months later isn't even compatible with the Internet speed that's rolling out. The paint selection that was last year's color of the year is now dated and tired. This is to say nothing of how the stock market or our incomes ebb and flow. So we must acknowledge that no matter how we slice Jesus's observation, He's right. The possessions we spend so much of our energy toiling for and worrying about cannot actually be possessed. And in a turn of irony, our possessions end up possessing us.

But once again Jesus brings us good news. We were created to value and cherish all that is worthy and enduring, that which cannot deteriorate or be stolen. These are the real treasures to be had, ones we can invest in now. Still, we wonder what these heavenly treasures actually are and how we can store them in heaven, a place we've never been to. We may also admit that sometimes the idea of heavenly treasures feels a bit detached from the lives we're living here on earth, where it's easier to get excited about a new light fixture or firepit.

So let's define our terms. Heavenly treasures consist of anything eternal in nature. When we teach our children about God and His ways, drop off chicken soup to encourage the sick or weary, give to the poor to the point of personal sacrifice, host a Bible study in our home, share a cup of tea with a friend, commit time to prayer, leverage our expertise and resources for our church communities, foster a child, talk to our neighbors and coworkers about the love and person of Jesus, and so on, we're storing up treasure in heaven. Put more simply, we store heavenly treasures when we spend ourselves for Christ and people.

What feels particularly ironic, and also urgent, is that we can only store up treasure in heaven from here on earth. This is our one shot. What an energizing thought that all the spinning and striving spent on vanishing possessions can be poured into what will not only matter in heaven but what matters now! Storing up treasure in heaven keeps us happily busy on earth where we have the privilege of depositing into people, which is far more lasting than depositing into up-and-down economies. We get to grow in Christ instead of growing in debt. We have the opportunity to invest in what will make us wealthy when we fly away, not in wealth that flies away. We get to invest in hearts over boats and end tables.

I think of Mary of Bethany who sat at Jesus's feet listening to what He said. While Martha's pots and pans urgently clanged from the kitchen, "What could be more important than this?"

"That which can never be taken from you," Jesus replied (Luke 10:42).

What will you do with today? How will you spend it? If you're spinning anxiously for what's temporal, redirect your energies toward Christ and the things dear to His heart, the heavenly treasures that can never be taken from you.

DAY 40

WHERE IS YOUR HEART?

"For where your treasure is, there your heart will be also."

Matthew 6:21

A FEW YEARS AGO, MUCH of my life's rhythms were disrupted. In a rather short time, I went from living at an allegro's tempo, to more of a ballad, and on bad days, a dirge. Some of the changes were thrust upon me (worldwide pandemics have a tendency to shut down large gatherings by which I made a chunk of my living) and some were chosen (I discovered what I'd long suspected—I thoroughly enjoy being home). But change is change, and the slower pace, the unrippled stillness, allowed for emotions and internal battles to be easily identifiable bubbles popping open at the surface. Moreover, I wasn't out "producing" like I had been. It's easy to justify not dealing with areas of pride, competition, selfishness, or hurt lurking in your heart because you're just too busy out "blessing people."

These quieter months, somewhat imposed upon me, have been ones of necessary reflection. I've needed the time to examine what I treasure. Perhaps you do too. This is important because our heart and our treasure share the same address. They're inseparable companions. Moving at breakneck speed at the altar of busyness obscures this understanding. So I've been giving this consideration. What do I spend my time on? What do my credit card statements tell me is important to me? What do my activities say about what matters most? Am I seeking a seat at the important tables or the ones where I can serve? When I'm busy, do I long to be in Christ's presence through prayer and His Word? When I close my eyes at night, are my imaginations populated only with what brings me personal pleasure, or am I also thinking about ways I can bless others? What we cherish reveals where our hearts reside.

When our lives are oriented around heavenly, eternal treasures, our hearts can rest. We labor hard, but what we labor for is secure in Christ. This stands to reason. Jesus has already settled that treasures stored in heaven cannot be stolen, nor can they deteriorate. But when we build our homes on Material Possessions Boulevard, we live in a state of anxiety, constantly striving to protect what might be taken from us, toiling to keep a step ahead of the competition. Our hearts are anxious because, at that address, nothing is guaranteed. So it's not just a factual matter that our hearts reside where our treasures do but also that what we deeply value sets the tone of our heart's environment. One is peaceful; the other frenzied and exhausting.

If your heart has become lost to you, you can find it, Jesus says. All you have to do is go to where your treasure is, and your heart is sure to be there. It can't be anywhere else. And if you find it in the wrong place, which we all do, sometimes several times in a day, we can ask the Lord to help us love a different treasure. He can transform the desires of our hearts (Ps. 37:4). He's done it in my own life in ways I thought positively impossible. Where I have treasured notoriety, I am now more inclined to cherish quiet impact or, as Jesus describes it, bearing fruit that lasts. Where having money has been my security, being generous with it has become my blessing. I could go on to describe the ways Christ has changed the things I love (which is saying something, because I came out of the womb ready to tap dance into just about every room this world has to offer).

If your heart is fretful, easily angered, too busy for anyone's agenda but your own, perhaps these are mere symptoms of loving the wrong things.

Jesus, help us love what You love. Change what we treasure so we can change the environments our hearts dwell in. We want Your rest. We want Your security. We want all that can never be taken from us.

DAY 41

GENEROSITY AND A LOT OF LIGHT

"The eye is the lamp of the body. If your eye is healthy, your whole body will be full of light. But if your eye is bad, your whole body will be full of darkness. So if the light within you is darkness, how deep is that darkness!"

Matthew 6:22–23

Before studying the Sermon on the Mount in any depth, I mostly understood its general ideas, though certainly not grasping some of its far-reaching theological truths (I'm convinced Jesus's Sermon is inexhaustible). But whenever I got to this illustration about healthy eyes and bad ones, light inside you being darkness, I would just throw up my hands. Not only was the metaphor lost on me, but it seemed to come out of nowhere, awkwardly wedging itself between two other metaphors—one about heaven and earth, the other about God and money. I was much relieved when one esteemed professor suggested that how this passage fits "is not immediately apparent to the modern reader."[60] *Phew!* I, the modern reader, exclaimed.

Jesus is using a cultural illustration the people of the day would have understood. Metaphorically, "the eye was as a window between a person's inside and outside."[61] It is like a lamp because when open and healthy, light floods our whole bodies; but when closed, suddenly our hands can't dice an onion, our feet can't safely cross the street. When the eye is light, so is the whole body; the same is true when the eye is dark. This makes sense but leads to another obscure part of the metaphor—healthy eyes versus bad ones. According to many trusted thinkers, there's a strong argument for "healthy" meaning whole, singly devoted, as well as generous and kind; "bad" meaning evil, stingy or greedy.[62] Now we're getting somewhere.

Here's a helpful translation: "The eye is the lamp of the body. Therefore, if your eye is whole and generous then your whole body will be enlightened. But if your eye is evil and greedy then your whole body will be darkened. Thus, if the light that is in you is darkness, what darkness that is!"[63]

We can now see how Jesus is setting forth living in the light versus living in darkness, much as He juxtaposed heaven and earth and will do the same with God and possessions. When we store up treasures in heaven, they are safe. When we live generously, light floods our beings and illumines our paths. We see this at work all around us. The wisest Christians I know, the ones who can see where life is headed, whose instincts are keen to what matters most, are the generous ones. I have yet to come across a charitable fool. But we have all watched smart people, shrewd businessmen and women, make the most reckless decisions driven by greed. Their world closes in on them as they choose self-indulgence over generosity. Sometimes they lose family members and dear relationships, whole careers, as they stumble in greed's darkness.

What a wonderful opportunity Jesus has set before us. We can choose to live in the light by living openhanded because all the treasures that matter are safe in Christ. As healthy eyes give light to our hands and feet, so kind and generous living illumines the other areas of our lives. The nature of a generous life is one lived in light of God's inexhaustible ability to provide. It celebrates sharing with our neighbors because Christ has shared Himself and His riches with us.

Lord, we want to see what matters. We don't want to be deceived by the endless pursuit of having more and more. Instead, we want to lead generous lives where we long to bless others because we know we never lack with You as Provider. We want to pull back the curtains and live in the light.

DAY 42

A GOOD MASTER AND A TERRIBLE ONE

"No one can serve two masters, since either he will hate one and love the other, or he will be devoted to one and despise the other. You cannot serve both God and money."

Matthew 6:24

Sometimes we live within the illusion that life is manageable and under our control. Having money and possessions can give us this misguided sense. And in some ways money does expand our ability to control outcomes, this perhaps being the main reason we make it our master. Although we don't ever actually call money by that name, we just live like it. But what we have in the bank and the material possessions we own start running on fumes when facing the things "money can't buy." I don't have to list them. We know what they are.

Jesus addresses this problem first by challenging one of our deep-seated assumptions—that it's possible to serve both God and money. He knew we would spend our whole lives trying to do just that. We live for God and the American Dream; God plus a thriving economy; God, if our comforts and securities are being met; God, only in health and companionship. If God is our Master only when money and possessions are leading the charge, He is no Master at all. This is what Jesus is telling us. We only get to have one.

My eighty-eight-year-old neighbor Miss Corrine called out to me from her front stoop. "Kelly, where *have* you been?" she asked deliberately, southernly. "I haven't seen you in for-*ev*-er." It might have been the cold weather that had kept our paths from crossing, but this day was beautiful and balmy, attempting to make good on spring's promises. I've never been terribly skilled at hiding my emotions, so I took the opportunity, on the altar of her front steps, to share what was weighing on me. "Kelly," she replied, "God is always working, even when you don't understand it." And then, smiling widely, arms extended on both sides, she said, "Just stretch out in Him."

I plodded home thinking, *Well, leave it to Miss Corrine to just nail Matthew 6:24 in five words.* See, money (and what it can buy) doesn't let us stretch out in it. We're either toiling for more of it, or if we happen to have it, we're trying to protect it or get even more than we already have, because the strange thing about money is you can never have enough. But our heavenly Father, the one who "owns the cattle on a thousand hills," who has given us the fullness of His riches in Christ, who never sleeps or slumbers, . . . we can stretch out in Him.

This very soul rest is at stake. Which is why Jesus's language here is strong and all-encompassing—it is impossible to serve both God and money. To "serve" is literally "to be a slave of."[64] It has to do with ownership. And lest we think we are the ones in charge of our money and possessions as opposed to the other way around, all we have to do is think about the ways money and stuff can own us, control our time, govern our decisions, rob our sleep. But if we give our lives to Jesus by serving Him, loving Him with single devotion, caring for what He cares for, we are resting in His ownership, living out our belongingness to Him.

Oh my friend, Jesus is not staging a grand duel between God and money, making us choose because He's threatened. He's singling out our idols. He's saying, "If you choose to serve the master of possessions, it will have your heart." What's more, you will ultimately end up recoiling from God and His ways because at different junctures in our lives God and money have competing agendas. But if your heavenly Father is the voice you trust, the one you harken to, the wholly good Master you choose to obey above all others, He will have your heart.

The original audience of Jesus's day would have heard the familiar peals of the first commandment, "You shall have no other gods before me" (Exod. 20:3 ESV), ringing out in His words. Much like the ancient idols of Israel who were powerless compared to Yahweh, our money and all it can buy is similarly worthless, especially when we consider what it chiefly cannot do—love us.

Heavenly Father, we don't want the limited and tiring god of money and materialism to be our master. We want to love You and be devoted to You. We trust You to meet our needs, to overflow the abundance of Your presence to us so we can live freely for Your purposes and restfully enough to stretch out in You.

DAY 43

CONSIDER THE BIRDS

"Therefore I tell you: Don't worry about your life, what you will eat or what you will drink; or about your body, what you will wear. Isn't life more than food and the body more than clothing? Consider the birds of the sky: They don't sow or reap or gather into barns, yet your heavenly Father feeds them. Aren't you worth more than they?"

Matthew 6:25–26

It was 3:30 in the morning. I was awake and restless, my mind racing as it sometimes does at this most inconvenient hour. Certain realities of life that had mostly felt concrete were suddenly gone or simply up in the air. Where will it all land? *No one knows*, the professionals kept saying. My mind flitted about from worry to prayer, not landing in either place for long. The birds chirped outside my window like it was the lunch hour. *Don't they know it's the middle of the night!* I wondered with ire.

Scientists call this early morning bird singing the dawn chorus. It's most noticeable in spring when birds are migrating or mating. *Dawn chorus* sounds so delightful except when you're trying to sleep in the middle of troubles and concerns. And yet, maybe this was part of the point Jesus was making: when your treasure is in heaven, your life full of light, and the One you serve is your heavenly Father, you can sing in the middle of a storm, reap during times of scarcity, stay on mission.

Birds were a wonderfully accessible illustration on the Galilean hillside where Jesus taught. We can envision a seagull gracefully soaring by or maybe skidding onto the water's surface after having digested a generous portion of freshly caught fish. We can hear Jesus say, *Consider, observe, look intently at what you see.* He wanted His disciples to stop and think about these winged creatures, specifically how they are fed despite not being able to do three important things for themselves: sow, reap, and store, each requiring the ability to plan.

When it comes to how you and I nourish ourselves and ultimately survive, we rely on all three. At least we rely on the farmers who rely on them. When I sow seeds in my garden, I check the seed packet for how many days to maturity so I know when I can reap the spinach, kale, and Japanese eggplant. Sadly, my little raised beds don't produce enough for me to store in barns (I'll let you know when I've reached that milestone), but if I could store, I would. Point being, we humans have the faculties to plan, save, and freeze the ground beef until we need it for lasagna. We sow seeds of higher education to secure better jobs, gain interest on our investments, build retirement we hope one day to reap. The birds cannot do this. They live simply, day-to-day, worm-to-worm (ne'er was there a more pleasant thought). Despite their lack of planning capabilities, they are fed, they are nourished, they have enough for their chicks.

How is this possible? we wonder. Because they have a heavenly Father who feeds them. And that heavenly Father isn't just the Father of the birds; He is *your* heavenly Father. And how much more are you worth to Him than the cardinals, starlings, robins, and blue jays? The obvious answer, *infinitely more.*

If what you sowed recently disappeared, what you reaped is no longer enough to be stored into barns, or your savings for tomorrow is being consumed today out of necessity, you can have confidence in your Father who promises to take care of you. So much assurance that in the middle of the night, in the middle of unprecedented times, when you hear the birds chirping with purpose and delight, you can join the hallelujahs of the dawn chorus. If He gives the birds reason to sing, how much more will He give you?

Heavenly Father, I place my anxieties about the future in Your sovereign care. I trust You to nourish and provide for me and my loved ones because I am worth more to You than the creatures for whom You daily provide. I thankfully receive what You have given me today and trust You will bring what's needed tomorrow.

DAY 44

WOULD YOU LOOK AT THOSE FLOWERS

"And why do you worry about clothes? Observe how the wildflowers of the field grow: They don't labor or spin thread. Yet I tell you that not even Solomon in all his splendor was adorned like one of these. If that's how God clothes the grass of the field, which is here today and thrown into the furnace tomorrow, won't he do much more for you—you of little faith?"

Matthew 6:28–30

My six-year-old niece Holland and I sat discussing what I should buy her brother Emmett for his tenth birthday. "Video game gift cards!" she said. "He loves playing video games, but . . ." her enthusiasm swiftly gave way to disapproval, "This is a want, not a need! Emmett doesn't *need* video games; he just *wants* them." (I'm not sure where Holland got the idea that asking for what you want on your birthday is cause for concern, but I credit her strong opinions.)

My dad overheard the conversation and joined our discussion. "Holland, what would you say is the difference between a want and a need?"

"Well," she said, "a need is water, and food, and my clothes, but a want is"—she paused as she considered her list of desires—"crayons, my coloring books, things like that."

"Very good Hollsy!" my dad affirmed. "You've got a good grasp on the difference between wants and needs."

We adults intellectually know the difference, but I'm not sure we don't confuse the two as often as children—our wants feel like needs. We have not, as Paul said, learned the secret of how to be content in all circumstances (Phil. 4:12). I think this is especially true for those of us whose most essential needs are regularly met. This condition leaves us hungering solely for what we want. For Jesus's original audience, though, most were yearning for fundamental provisions, such as food and clothing; hence Jesus's illustrations about nourished birds and well-dressed flowers. We must keep this context in mind as we seek to apply His words to our current situations.

Jesus encourages us to *observe* the wildflowers, or *learn, examine closely*.[65] When is the last time you sat for a moment and reflected on flowers in a field, or from your cut garden, or—let's keep it real—the grocery store? If we consider the birds in the same hour that we observe the flowers, we'll remember that flowers are even less capable than birds at providing for themselves. Birds can fly and gather food and build nests; flowers cannot sew fabric or toil for the money necessary to purchase a new spring dress and yet our heavenly Father clothes them. And He doesn't throw any old drab thing on them as though they are orphans at the mercy of a miserly caretaker. Each is adorned more splendidly than the wisest, wealthiest king in Israel's storied history, Solomon.

Jesus says, *Examine that.*

He then uses "lesser to greater" reasoning which was a common way to make an argument in ancient Jewish culture. He asserts, if God exquisitely clothes the wildflowers (lesser), with how much more lavish care will He clothe you and me (greater)? As New Testament believers, Jesus's words take on added meaning. Not only does our heavenly Father meet our physical needs, but the Holy Spirit supplies us with a wardrobe of compassion, goodness, humility, gentleness, and patience (Col. 3:12)—garments that cannot be purchased, that never go out of style, that make us exceedingly attractive and distinguished for God's glory.

So hover over a blooming tulip or a freshly budding rose and observe its beauty and what it didn't exert to be so splendidly dressed. The reflection will lead you to its desired end: a confident rest in your heavenly Father's ability and desire to clothe you with even greater dignity and splendor (both physical and spiritual). Perhaps then you will find that you don't really need some of what you've wanted and what you never knew you wanted, He wants to give you. We can then joyfully say alongside Paul, "If we have food and clothing, we will be content with these" (1 Tim. 6:8)!

DAY 45

THE WEAKNESS OF WORRY

"Can any of you add one moment to his life span by worrying? . . . Therefore don't worry about tomorrow, because tomorrow will worry about itself. Each day has enough trouble of its own."

Matthew 6:27, 34

I CAN'T EVER RECALL A time when in the middle of a stressful season I said to a friend, *I feel so much better this morning; thank goodness I was up worrying all night.* I'm not sure why we often default to worrying when we know it can't achieve a single thing. I suppose worrying makes us feel like we're getting ahead of a possible pain, fallout, or loss we fear is coming down the pike. We know getting out in front won't stop whatever we're worrying about from hitting us, but at least we won't be ambushed by it. At best, worry is a lousy form of preparation and usually a terrible waste of energy since half the time the stuff we worry about never happens anyway.

This is what Jesus is detailing for us in these verses. Worrying can't lengthen our lives by even a moment (or add an inch to our height, which I could have used while playing basketball in high school). And there's no need for us to stew about what troubles might come tomorrow because we have enough to concern ourselves with today. Worrying about what may or may not happen in the future only snatches the precious moments we have right now, the only moments we're assured of. If we prayerfully and responsibly deal with today's troubles, instead of squandering the time fretting about tomorrow's, we might actually be able to keep certain ones from snowballing into yet another day.

Jesus is offering us valuable, commonsense truths that stand on their own, but how much more meaningful when we remember who it is speaking them![66] That the Son of God Himself is the One relieving us of worry transforms His words from mere wisdom statements to life-changing kingdom of heaven realities because of His presence in our lives. We all know that living a life flooded with worry is awful and fruitless, but much of the time we can't help it. What we need is to be rescued from it. That rescue is what so much of Jesus's Sermon is about. Because the presence of Christ has infiltrated our world, He not only teaches us how but also empowers us to live free of debilitating anxiety.

What is keeping you up at night? Where have your resources fallen short of what you need? Who is threatening your possessions? I could tell you, *Don't worry because that's inadequate and not very smart,* but that wouldn't help you. What is needed are Jesus's anchoring truths about how the hurting are the flourishing ones because the kingdom of heaven belongs to them and how your heavenly Father knows what you need and is not caught off guard by your concerns. You don't have to get out in front of what might happen because He's already there.

Worry doesn't get to have a bedroom in the Father's house where daily bread is provided and needs tended. Worry is an outsider in a world where God's people are infinitely more looked after than birds who can't meal-plan yet are fed, where flowers that can't slip into dresses or tuxedos are adorned in glory. And at the bottom of all this, we need not worry because Jesus is present among us. He is with us. He is with *you.* And the inexhaustible riches of His glory are present to meet your needs.

Heavenly Father, you feed the birds and clothe the flowers, and still I am much more valuable to You. Relieve me from worrying, not only because it's tiresome and fruitless but because it's needless in Your presence. Supply me with Your provision, help me remember You are eager to meet my needs, and generously give me Yourself. Let me go throughout my day, not oblivious to my real concerns but anxious to place them in Your care.

DAY 46

WHAT TO SEEK FIRST

"So don't worry, saying, 'What will we eat?' or 'What will we drink?' or 'What will we wear?' For the Gentiles eagerly seek all these things, and your heavenly Father knows that you need them. But seek first the kingdom of God and his righteousness, and all these things will be provided for you."

Matthew 6:31–33

The kingdom of heaven reprioritizes our ambitions and concerns. Instead of our minds spinning anxiously about all the unknowns and what-ifs, Jesus said to His disciples, *That's the kind of stuff the Gentiles concern themselves with.* Jesus knew that bringing the Gentiles into the discussion would be a healthy motivator, like when your friend used to tell you in high school to stop wearing those weird shoes because you might look like "that group" who was clearly headed downhill, fate sealed in the ninth grade.

Jesus, of course, wasn't being pompous or unkind; He was simply making an observation. The Jews saw the Gentiles as religious outsiders, pagans who didn't worship the God of Israel. Their lives were naturally characterized by scheming and anxiety because their gods were fickle. Having their needs met was unpredictable at best. In notable contrast, followers of Jesus are under the warm and generous care of our heavenly Father who isn't oblivious to our needs or powerless to meet them. Whereas the Gentiles had to inform their gods of what they needed, our God will never be caught nervously perspiring because if only He had known that you wanted to be married, He would have made sure you sat next to that fantastic person in chemistry; or if He'd been aware of your financial situation, He could have arranged for that promotion.

Jesus speaks a word of rest into all this anxiety—*the Father already knows what you need.*

Since we're free as Christ followers—truly, absolutely, not just in theory but in practice, *free*—to lay in His care the worries we have about our finances, children, health, home repairs, relationships, future, we can pour ourselves into pursuing God's kingdom and His righteousness. And this is where the real adventure begins, our lives postworry.

Seeking first God's kingdom and righteousness can feel like ethereal terms we don't always envision interlacing with the rough and tumble of work, raising a family, investing our money, making dinner, dealing with singleness. But when we think, in the simplest terms, of God's kingdom as the place of His rule and reign, and His righteousness as His will and what He values, we can see how His "kingdom" and "righteousness" infiltrate all of life. Instead of these being separate and detached endeavors from our "real lives," they're priorities that transform our lives.

As Dallas Willard says, seeking first His kingdom is about placing "top priority on identifying and involving [ourselves] in what God is doing and in the kind of righteousness he has."[67] When we do this, he says, "all else needed is provided." This is the joy and rest that comes from seeking the desires of our Father's heart first. When we put our own agenda at the top, let our personal passions run roughshod over obedience to Christ, this is when we live like "Gentiles"—anxious, tired, striving, stressed. I wish I didn't know so much about this.

When you wake up in the morning, who or what do you long for? As you drive into work, knead bread, help a little one out the door to school, or go out to eat with friends, what is most important to you in those moments? Does your heart, in work and rest, simmer with love for God and what matters to Him? For certain, seeking God's rule and righteousness will mean activities like Bible study, prayer, worship, missions, generosity, and being part of your local church, but these will flow from a heart that has surrendered its own agenda for that of Christ's—a heart that has put His will and ways above its own.

C. S. Lewis famously said, "Aim at Heaven and you will get Earth 'thrown in': aim at Earth and you will get neither."[68] What is your heart's aim?

DAY 47

WHAT IT MEANS TO JUDGE

"Do not judge, so that you won't be judged. For you will be judged by the same standard with which you judge others, and you will be measured by the same measure you use."

Matthew 7:1–2

Over the past few days, Jesus has helped us loosen our death grip on money and possessions so we can store enduring treasure, He's disrupted our personal agendas for His kingdom purposes, and He's gotten after us—in the kindest way—about all the needless worrying we do. But I wonder if He hasn't saved the most challenging part for last—what it means to discern sin in another's life without condemnation, to disagree without judgment, to address the darkness in our own lives first.

I'm in seminary, and one of my assignments is working with a mentor to help me grow in the quality of gentleness. My friend Chris, who agreed to be my mentor, met me for lunch to discuss what gentleness and patience look like, in particular when people frustrate you so intensely you see stars (not that I ever get this worked up). As we conversed about these virtues, Chris told me that from his earliest memory he has wanted the person sitting across from him to win. "It's just the way God made me," he explained. Chris's desire for others to be the best they can be in Christ is perhaps the kingdom antithesis to judging one another. I haven't stopped thinking about it. We can't pick people apart, harshly judging their motives, dissecting their every move at the same time we're cheering for them to succeed.

So I wonder if Jesus doesn't want us to start there. If He doesn't want us to ask ourselves what we want, at a heart level, for the person we're judging. Do we want them to flourish as a child of God, or do we delight in their failures and idiosyncrasies as if we're on an Easter egg hunt cracking open their sins? So often we point the finger at someone not because we're genuinely concerned for their well-being but because it props up our own sense of self-righteousness. And if that person has wounded us, discovering one of their shortcomings is yet another egg in our basket. Unjust judgment is a vicious cycle that puffs up the judge and offers zero assistance to the person being judged. It's not the way of Christ's kingdom, which is founded on grace, mercy, forgiveness, forbearance, and wanting others to prosper in Jesus.

Of course, "do not judge" does not mean we forsake the important spiritual responsibility of discerning between right and wrong. It doesn't mean we stop making moral judgments or calling sin "sin" and goodness "good." Jesus will soon talk about how necessary it is to be able to differentiate between sheep and wolves (Matt. 7:15–20). When people say, "Don't judge me," what they often mean is they will accept nothing less than your approving their every choice and behavior, and this isn't what Jesus means based on the rest of His teachings.

The following is a needed insight: being morally discerning is not the same thing as being personally condemning.[69] We must discern sinful behavior, but we need never stand in ultimate condemnation of a person. That is to stand in the place of God. James reminds us that Jesus is the only and final Judge (James 4:11–12).

Today let's give grace. Let's draw from the love and mercy of Jesus, who does not repay us with the measure we deserve, who laid down His life for us on the cross, bearing our judgment so we might have life (2 Cor. 5:21)! Who might do better with your encouragement instead of your criticism? Whose strengths can you look to bolster in lieu of exploiting their weaknesses? Whom do you want to win?

DAY 48

OF BEAMS AND SPLINTERS

"Why do you look at the splinter in your brother's eye but don't notice the beam of wood in your own eye? Or how can you say to your brother, 'Let me take the splinter out of your eye,' and look, there's a beam of wood in your own eye? Hypocrite! First take the beam of wood out of your eye, and then you will see clearly to take the splinter out of your brother's eye."

Matthew 7:3–5

I GREW UP IN A pastor's home, and this meant being well acquainted with culturally odd metaphors like having beams in your eye while other people had tiny splinters. My dad did a good job of teaching me and my siblings that we have eagle eyes when it comes to spotting one another's sin, but when it comes to seeing our own, we have these things called blind spots. And he really hammered that home. It's been one of the most well-worn pieces of wisdom I've carried throughout my life.

While large beams and minuscule specks of wood dust may not be part of our everyday worlds, for Jesus this was shoptalk. Two siblings working alongside each other as carpenters was a familiar setting for His audience.[70] We can imagine how silly a scene it would be if one brother pointed out a piece of sawdust in the other's eye while having a plank in his own. (We have an updated version of this: the pot calling the kettle black.) Or how dangerous it might have been if Big Beam Brother tried to remove Little Splinter Brother's speck while his own vision was alarmingly obscured? Jesus says that this is what it means to be a hypocrite.

As we saw yesterday, the problem isn't employing godly discernment to determine matters of sin and righteousness in another person, it's that we often do so while totally oblivious to our own issues of materialism, arrogance, selfishness, smugness, sexual immorality, anger. . . . The Pharisees of Jesus's day were notorious for this. They kept the letter of the law to a T but had no problem cheating their parents out of financial support or throwing a blind man out of the temple for having the gall to be healed on the Sabbath. Jesus described them as blind guides who would strain a gnat from their drinking water but then go swallow a camel (Matt. 23:24).

But if we keep talking in terms of planks, specks, camels, gnats, we may miss how present these tendencies are for us in our modern-day Christian relationships. Our propensity to judge smaller sins in others while we harbor big ones is exactly what causes so many tragic divisions. We judge people's politics, parenting, the vacations they take, all while not honestly assessing our own unhealthy attachments and idols. So, what are we to do about this human proclivity to use 3D glasses when viewing another Christian's faults while viewing our own through a blindfold? Jesus tells us plainly: remove the colossal beam that's blocking your vision.

The only way I know how to do this is to go to the foot of the cross. It's the single place I know where you and I can clearly see our sin and freshly appreciate Christ's forgiveness and grace. It's where the light beam of God's holiness pierces the wood beam of our self-righteousness so we can suddenly see. Only then do we have clear vision to perceive what temptations or sins might be tripping up a brother or sister. But notice what Jesus says is the purpose of this restored vision. It's not so we can more accurately judge people up and down but so we can help them. How about that for an unexpected turn of events?

Is there someone who's sin you can't stop seeing? Are you focused on their issues so you don't have to deal with your own? Have you lost sight of the sin in your own heart and subsequently the sacrifice of Christ on your behalf? If so, go to the cross. Only then will you see with keen enough eyes the sins of your brother or sister in order that healing might come for them too.

DAY 49

OF PEARLS AND PIGS

"Don't give what is holy to dogs or toss your pearls before pigs, or they will trample them under their feet, turn, and tear you to pieces."

Matthew 7:6

I'M NOT SURE WHEN IS the most opportune time to bring up things like snarling dogs and pigs running off with pearls. If you haven't brewed your coffee or tea yet, I would go get that mug. These images are not nearly as calming or endearing as Jesus's earlier illustrations of frolicking birds chirping in the trees and vibrant flowers swaying in the wind. Not to mention, the metaphors aren't as easily interpreted. But I do think there's enough undisputed wisdom here that can positively affect our relationships if we'll heed Jesus's words. This single verse has, in fact, helped me respond differently than I naturally would have to some of the dearest people in my life. His wisdom has preserved some of my most precious relationships. I pray it will be as meaningful for you.

The first thing we must know is that Jesus is not being mean-spirited or prejudiced toward "lesser" people. This would go against what He's already taught about loving our enemies, going the extra mile, and being generous. Though "dogs" and "pigs" stood for the despised in Jewish culture and "pearls" and "what is holy" for what was prized, Jesus uses these cultural realities to teach us something important. Perhaps for the original audience, it meant waiting to take the gospel to the Gentiles until after the resurrection.[71] Or not wasting precious energy trying to force other Jews to believe Jesus's message when they didn't want any part of it.[72]

Since you and I live on the other side of Jesus's death and resurrection, and since He has commissioned us to tell the people we know all about Him, His teaching may give us a newly realized application. Dallas Willard suggested that the main idea here is not to force upon people what is useless to them.[73] A pig would not appreciate a pearl necklace you clasped around its neck for a special birthday, except in a cartoon, which I think could be cute. And your adorable puppy or a snaggle-toothed wild dog would have no use for a Bible study on Hebrews. She wants your leftover rib eye.

As Christ followers, we need the Holy Spirit to help us walk this fine line. On one side our moral discernment can turn into unfair judgment of others, but on the other side we can be guilty of not being discerning at all, forcing pearls on pigs who don't want them. This doesn't mean we retreat from sharing the good news of the gospel or speaking truth that might cost us. But what this passage has revealed about my own heart is that sometimes I use God's truth to control others. I might want something for them that is especially good and godly—something plainly biblical—but stating my thoughts about it over and over and twisting their arm, it turns out, isn't that effective. I've tried this a lot of ways. And it can actually have the reverse effect.

Goodness, sometimes we even go the subtler routes of sending an article that talks about how good church or Bible study is for a person's mental health, or why voting for a certain politician makes the most biblical sense. But these kinds of approaches actually belie our lack of faith in God's capable ability to draw our loved ones to Himself, to convict at the right time. The much more effective approach is meeting with our heavenly Father in our secret place *first*, placing our loved ones in His care. And then watching with expectation not for our agenda to be accomplished in their lives but His.

Heavenly Father, we give You those closest to us and those we long to reach with Your love. Give us the discernment to know when to speak Your truth. And once spoken, give us the restraint to hold back pearls until they'll be most appreciated. May we trust You with those we love by praying instead of manipulating.

DAY 50

OUR GOD IS RELATIONAL

"Ask, and it will be given to you. Seek, and you will find. Knock, and the door will be opened to you. For everyone who asks receives, and the one who seeks finds, and to the one who knocks, the door will be opened."

Matthew 7:7--8

I suppose that before we reflect further on the idea of asking and receiving, seeking and finding, knocking and doors being opened, we should go ahead and address the elephant that often plops himself down in the middle of our prayer rooms bearing the big conundrum: *If God already knows what we need, why do we have to ask Him for it?*

When we think in these terms, which is natural to do, God can come off as aloof at best. Here He is, sitting on everything we need, but if we don't come begging, He's not going to give it to us. But this just isn't the picture Jesus paints of our heavenly Father. He has already revealed details of God's care and provision for us, even for the most delicate hummingbird and fragile wildflower. So a few things to consider . . .

First, and go with me down this rabbit hole, what if your Father in heaven *didn't* know what you needed? That would really be something. You'd be left babbling like the Gentiles for His attention, scrambling to have your needs met, hoping He saw the urgent note you left Him. If God is worth His salt, He can be nothing less than all-knowing (an attribute known as *omniscience*).

Second, we sometimes think it unkind that God would want us to ask, seek, and knock. Why doesn't He just hand things over? If we think about this for long enough, though, we might be in awe of how much He gives us that we haven't asked for. A special friend you didn't know you needed, a fulfilling career shift you hadn't planned, a stretch of time where not *one* of the people in your household was sick and life just hummed along as it should, a sermon that hit your heart at just the right time and in just the right way, an invitation to someone's beach house who just wanted you to have it for the week (this actually has not happened to me, but nonetheless). . . . He is constantly showering us with provisions, necessities, and gifts we weren't seeking. He is good to us even when we don't ask Him to be.

Third, these three active pursuits are the polar opposite of resignation. I was talking with my friend Joan about a certain area of my life that has been disappointing. I told her that after praying over it for months I was just resigned to whatever God wanted to do. But really what I was saying is that I was tired of engaging with Him about it. I had essentially given up. Joan knowingly smiled at me in the way that only a longtime follower of Christ can and said, "But don't stop hoping. You know God wants you to expect good things from Him, even while you're waiting." It was a loving prod to keep pursuing Him in prayer, even if it felt unproductive.

Fourth, we must consider that asking, seeking, and knocking are relational actions. I don't knock on a door if I know my friend is not there. I don't set my plants down on my kitchen island and say to them, *Look! I have a favor to ask. . . .* And whenever I'm on a desperate hunt that requires me to seek with all my energy, it's either for a person (like when my nieces and nephews would slip out of my sight in their toddler years) or a thing attached to a person (like a wedding ring that goes missing). How terribly tragic it would be if God did not give us the relational gift of being able to ask, seek, and knock. He would be nothing more than the delivery person we hardly ever see dropping packages of daily bread on our front doorstep.

Prayer is not a merely transactional affair; it is a relational one. And what says more about loving relationships than asking, seeking, and knocking? If prayer were only about getting what we want, it would be cold and cumbersome. But if it's about intimacy with the living God, then these pursuits show the relationship is alive.

So as you sit in the tall grass on that hillside, hearing these words from Jesus, remember that your Savior *deeply* knows what it feels like to ask ardently, seek tirelessly, and knock persistently. He is not asking you to do something He has not already done. He has gone before you to show you what such a vibrant relationship with the Father looks like.

Dear friend, to do the same is not only to enjoy a rich relationship with your Father but to become more like His Son. So, what do you want from God? Have you asked Him for it? Are you willing to seek Him with the passion of one who is after a hidden treasure? Will you knock with expectation, knowing He opens all good doors in His time? This is what it means to be in relationship. It is about so much more than getting what we want; it's about finding out that what we've always wanted is Him.

DAY 51

OUR GOD IS RESPONSIVE

"Ask, and it will be given to you. Seek, and you will find. Knock, and the door will be opened to you. For everyone who asks receives, and the one who seeks finds, and to the one who knocks, the door will be opened."

Matthew 7:7–8

One of my favorite Old Testament professors, Dr. Knut Heim, sent me an email and closed it with an exhortation: "As you continue to serve the Lord and your neighbors, ask not what you can do for God, but what He can do for you." At first I thought, *Well, this sounds like really terrible theology*. And then I noticed he referenced Matthew 7:7–8 in parenthesis. Like a good professor, he wanted me to contend with the text, and the text is indeed an invitation to seek God for what He can give us.

Jesus has already affirmed that our heavenly Father is caring, all the way down to a hummingbird's breakfast and a lily's sundress. He's the giver of good gifts like the sun's warmth, rain showers, and daily bread. He is compassionate and competent, so we need not worry. He is personal, relational, all-knowing. And today Jesus tells us something more: our God is responsive. What else can we gather from One who gives to those who ask, is found by those who seek Him, and opens doors for those who knock?

I hope you will sit with this for a moment. I hope you will allow this truth to plant itself in the middle of your prayer garden, the one where pesky weeds of doubts and unanswered prayers also grow. It's okay. Let it all spring up together for now. If you don't, you'll end up setting this remarkable passage aside because you just don't know what to do with it. All of us have asked God for things we didn't receive, looked hard for what we still haven't found, and knocked on doors that seem more like castle walls. This is where we're in good company, not only with countless saints but with Jesus Himself who did not get what He asked for when He prayed for the cup of the cross to pass from Him (Matt. 26:39).

It is true, God does not give us everything we ask for. That would make Him out to be our personal butler or cosmic concierge, as one of my pastors used to say. The image Jesus paints instead is that of a loving Father who responds to His children, who delights to engage. Responding to our pleas is not just what He does; it's indicative of who He is. Yes, there are times when our prayers require that frustrating state of being we refer to as *waiting*. Not all prayers are answered right away. I think that's part of what it means to seek and knock. Not so God can see how persistent we are; rather so we can discover how worth it He and the treasures we're seeking are. Other times we ask for what we consider good things, but still God says no because He can see what we can't. Our vision is too limited, too finite to behold the big picture. Remember when you begged God to give you someone or something, and then just a few years down the road you fell on your face thanking Him that He didn't give you what you asked for? His *nos* often prove His love for us just as much as His *yeses*.

There's also the problem of not receiving from God because we're praying for the wrong things—things that flow against the current of His kingdom and righteousness. (It's why my professor led with some of answered prayer's prerequisites: serving the Lord and our neighbors, which are will-of-God pursuits.) Other times we pray with wrong hearts. (At this point in our devotional we are well acquainted with the idea of right hearts and right actions working in tandem with each other.) At the same time, I wonder if N. T. Wright doesn't just nail it when he says that "for most of us, the problem is not that we are too eager to ask for the wrong things. The problem is that we are not eager enough to ask for the right things."[74] I have been guilty of this. Murmuring and slumping around the house because of all the things that aren't going well, things I am more willing to complain about instead of going to battle for.

Still, perhaps you have eagerly asked for the right things, the "will of God" things, and did not receive what you asked for. They may have even been life-and-death requests. Sometimes these unanswered prayers just need to be left growing in our prayer gardens until one day the Master Gardener explains it all to us. In the meantime, we say, *Lord, thank You that You are a God whose nature is to respond. Thank You that You are loving, trustworthy, and eager to engage with us when we pray. We come expectant. We come eager to be in Your presence because we know we will not be left alone there. And as much as we long to do things for You, as we seek Your righteousness, we are eager to know what You can do for us!*

DAY 52

OUR GOD IS GOOD

"Who among you, if his son asks him for bread, will give him a stone? Or if he asks for a fish, will give him a snake? If you then, who are evil, know how to give good gifts to your children, how much more will your Father in heaven give good things to those who ask him."

Matthew 7:9–11

One of the things that really stands out to me about the Sermon on the Mount is how much time Jesus gives to describing who God is. Have you thought about that? The Bible is full of prophets and petitioners, mothers and kings, fishermen and queens who wrote poems, prayers, sermons, and songs about the nature of God, but the Sermon offers us *Jesus's* perspective about Him.

Feels like we should lean in a little further.

In this passage (connected to verses 7–8 about asking, seeking, and knocking in prayer), Jesus wants us to know something important about our heavenly Father, something that is hard to believe about Him in our difficult and sometimes tragic world or when we desperately ask Him for things we haven't gotten or didn't get. It's something He knew we might be tempted to stop believing about God—that He is *good*.

My niece Lily is four. The other day she asked her mom for a second doughnut, and Megen kindly told her she needed to wait. Lily declared, "When I grow up, I'm gonna be really, really nice to my kids!"

"Really?" Megen said. "What does that mean?"

"Like, if my kid asks for doughnuts, I'm gonna say yes. If they ask to color or go play outside, I'm gonna say yes." After pausing a moment, Lily summed up her future as a parent: "I'm gonna be a yes mom."

Saying yes 100 percent of the time makes great sense to a four-year-old, but when Lily grows up, she will understand that being a yes mom will keep her from being a good mom. Being a giving mom, on the other hand, will make her a Christlike one.

The word *give* is mentioned five times in verses 7–11, portraying the nurturing aspect of God's good nature. Have you thought about this recently? That God is a giver? My friend Mary Katharine is the dominant gift-giver in my circle of friends and in turn loves good gifts herself, mostly the kind of stuff that is novel for about three months and then discreetly makes its way down the stairs and onto a shelf in her basement never to be seen again—an electric foot massager, an espresso maker, or my personal favorite, a gramophone for your smartphone. The gift-giving Jesus highlights in the first century is more earthy and rustic, and it wasn't stuff than ended up in the basement. But the illustration holds: He delights to give to you.

The crowds listening to Him were accustomed to their children asking for bread and fish. Jesus is not only showing that human parents want to give good gifts to their children but also that they don't want to deceive them. Think of how a brown-hued stone, if the light hits it just right, could appear as a round loaf of bread or how a slithering snake, if writhing just so, could come off as a flapping fish.[75] Once again, Jesus uses the "lesser to greater" argument here, revealing "how much more" our heavenly Father will give good things to those who ask Him. (Matthew says "good things," and Luke says "the Holy Spirit." What greater gift is there than the ever-present companion of the Holy Spirit who comes alongside you?)

Jesus here circles back around to the fundamentals: our heavenly Father loves to respond to His children. He delights to give us good things, even more than parents are eager to give good gifts to their children on Christmas morning. He would never deceive us or trick us by giving us something we thought was a blessing only to find out was a rock or a snake or a gramophone. He will not give us everything we ask for, but He will give what He deems best. This does not make Him a yes dad, but it makes Him a good and giving one.

Father, in our struggles to believe You are good in the middle of prayers that have yet to be answered the way we hope, or that were already answered in ways impossible to understand, help us to keep asking, seeking, knocking, all the while believing that You are a good, good Father.

DAY 53

THE GOLDEN RULE

"Therefore, whatever you want others to do for you, do also the same for them, for this is the Law and the Prophets."

Matthew 7:12

My favorite spin instructor recently said, in the nicest possible tone, "If anyone's standing in your path, move them out of the way." In fairness, she may have been talking about friends who want you to eat nachos with them instead of working out, but the sentiment isn't unusual. We hear some version of this all the time: *Look out for number one. Don't let anyone stand in the way of your dreams. If someone hurts you, don't get mad, get even.* It's just kind of the way we do things as humans. In perfect Sermon on the Mount form, Jesus turns this all upside down, telling us that if we really want to live the good life, we must love others.

Today's verse is one of the most beloved statements in Jesus's Sermon, so much so it has even crossed into spheres outside the Christian faith. It is the positive form of a similar saying that dates back to the time of Christ: "Don't do to others what you don't want them to do to you."[76] While it's true that Jesus frames commands both negatively and positively, in this case the positive framing makes all the difference. You don't have to do anything at all to accomplish the negative form of the Golden Rule.[77] As long as you're not doing something to someone that you don't want done to you, you can lie on your couch all day eating gummy worms and still hit that mark.

But think of the output, the outward focus, the pouring out on others the same care we wish for ourselves that Jesus's version of the

Golden Rule requires. It's the summary of the "greater righteousness" Jesus has been teaching all along.

The Golden Rule keeps us from loathing ourselves because it assumes we care about our own desires and well-being and that we have enough self-awareness to know the ways we long to be treated. At the same time, it keeps us from thinking too much about ourselves, redirecting our self-care to others-care.[78] Two of my close friends who work for JMI just returned from a dangerous part of the world to care for refugees fleeing the crosshairs of an unprovoked war. One left behind her fiancé and the other his family. My friends went at great cost to themselves not because they don't care about their own well-being but because they know that if they were the ones fleeing their homes, leaving loved ones behind, having no idea if they'd ever be able to return home, they would want someone to care for them. They believe Jesus's words are meant to be practiced in real life.

Jesus's beloved disciple, John, reminds us that the only way we're able to live according to the Golden Rule is because God has loved us first through Christ (1 John 4:10–11). If this weren't true, Jesus's teaching would be the Impossible Rule. He is the one and only fulfillment of all that the Law and the Prophets demand (Matt. 5:17), and because His love is shed abroad in our hearts, we are now empowered to love in a way few think normal or reasonable (Matt. 7:12).

Where does it feel impossible to care for someone else in the way you long to be cared for? Who are you struggling to love? C. S. Lewis says, "Do not waste time bothering whether you 'love' your neighbor; act as if you did. As soon as we do this we find one of the great secrets. When you are behaving as if you loved someone, you will presently come to love him."[79] So don't worry if you don't have feelings of love in the moment—feelings often follow actions. The One who has already fulfilled the Law and the Prophets is present with you, right in this moment, to walk with you in carrying out His love.

Father, we don't want to move people out of our way. We want to love those in and around our way with the same love we long to have for ourselves. Only in Jesus can this be accomplished. Help us love as You love.

DAY 54

THE ROAD THAT LEADS TO LIFE

"Enter through the narrow gate. For the gate is wide and the road broad that leads to destruction, and there are many who go through it. How narrow is the gate and difficult the road that leads to life, and few find it."

Matthew 7:13–14

I REMEMBER READING THESE VERSES as a kid and hearing them taught in church and Christian school. They had an ominous ring to them, at least partly because the terms didn't seem clear. If the wide gate and broad road that leads to a terrible end is the normal, obvious path that most people are on, how do I know I'm not on it? And what exactly is the narrow gate and the challenging road that leads to life? The stakes seem high and there's no "gospel message" here attached to Jesus's call. And a call it is. Jesus concludes His Sermon not with further instructions but by laying out two paths before us, inviting us, urging us, to choose the path of life.

This passage was often taught to me independent of the rest of Jesus's Sermon. I'm prayerful that after having walked through Jesus's teachings and seeing today's verses as a conclusion to them, His call will be less vague to us. When we look at the path most people are on, it's not pounded by a community longing to serve others in a way that penetrates the darkness and acts as salt preserving from decay. I don't know too many people who order their lives around storing up eternal treasures over material possessions and pleasures. Most on the broad road may not be for murder, adultery, or hatred, but how many are really committed to contending with anger and lust, are fighting for their marriages when it's inconvenient, are serious about loving their enemies, long to treat others the way they themselves want to be treated? Jesus's Sermon is full of "broad road" tendencies and "narrow gate" instructions.

If you, like me, believe salvation is achieved "by grace" alone "through faith alone" (Eph. 2:8–9), you might be concerned that this sounds like works-righteousness (earning our salvation by doing good works), but it's certainly not that. Jesus has already declared Himself the fulfillment of the Law and the Prophets. All the righteousness we lack in ourselves has been accomplished in Him. And in John 10:9, Jesus declares Himself as the gate through which we enter to access life in His kingdom both now and forever. But don't you think that if our lives have been transformed by Christ it will look like more than an invisible set of beliefs collecting dust in our heads? Praise God that Jesus wants not just heaven for us later but our whole lives and whole hearts right here and right now.

This passage used to terrify me because I was afraid I might not believe the right things enough and therefore miss the narrow gate. I hope you are not terrified. Jesus is inviting you to follow Him on the road that leads to life. But I do hope you are sobered by the call. Sobered because it's life-and-death-level serious that you've come to Him as King and as a natural outflow are doing the things He says to do. But I also hope you are energized. This is the only life that is truly worth living. The broad path is ultimately boring. It's paved with predictable cycles of worry, deteriorating possessions, striving, animosity, and even when everything is "just right," there's the fear of losing it all. And in the end, worse than mere boredom, it leads to death.

But the narrow gate requires a radical dependence that so closely knits our souls to Christ we cannot help but be transformed by His presence. It means walking with a community of people who love one another because Christ has loved us. It means intersecting with the broad path often enough for light to shine and salt to preserve.

So we do need to ask ourselves, Am I on the narrow road? Is my life organized around the will and ways of Jesus according to Scripture? Am I living for the same things the people on the wide road who don't know

Christ are living for, or am I daily desiring God and His righteousness first? Am I loving others as myself? These aren't kingdom-entrance exam questions; they merely help us know what road we're on.

Dear sojourner, if you're plodding alongside Jesus, if the path at times leads you uphill and leaves you feeling uprooted, while the well-traveled one appears paved with ease and pleasure, it can only mean one thing: you're on the right road.

DAY 55

WHO IS TRUE?

"Be on your guard against false prophets who come to you in sheep's clothing but inwardly are ravaging wolves. You'll recognize them by their fruit. Are grapes gathered from thornbushes or figs from thistles? In the same way, every good tree produces good fruit, but a bad tree produces bad fruit. A good tree can't produce bad fruit; neither can a bad tree produce good fruit. Every tree that doesn't produce good fruit is cut down and thrown into the fire. So you'll recognize them by their fruit."

Matthew 7:15–20

One year a friend gave me tiny melon seedlings to plant in my garden. I tucked them into the soil and eagerly awaited their growth. As their vines began to lengthen and leaves began to form, something seemed off. The plants were looking strangely tomato-like. It wasn't until actual fruit began to form that I realized my friend had given me not melons but Cherokee Purple tomatoes. This is the nature of fruit bearing: sometimes these realizations take time. The flip side, though, is that fruit doesn't lie. It points not only to the type of tree or plant from which it comes but also the substance of it, healthy or diseased.

Jesus takes these immutable agrarian principles and applies them to our ability to discern true Christ followers from false ones. So as we sit back down on that grassy slope, refreshed by the Galilean breeze, perhaps we can imagine Jesus gesturing to a fruit tree, offering us a visual. Just as a fig tree cannot bear anything but figs and a healthy tree will never bring about rotten fruit, so it is with the prophets. If a person claims to speak for God but their lives produce harm to others, divisiveness in relationships, half-truths that lead astray, greed that oppresses . . . well then, plain and simple, they cannot be of God.

Perhaps you trusted a spiritual leader only to be misled, used, or betrayed. This is a terribly disorienting and disillusioning experience because not only are you wounded by someone you believed to be a true Christ follower, but you feel as though you've also been wounded by God because the person acted in His name. I believe this is one of the reasons Jesus's warning is so strong here. He desperately wants us to be careful about whom we entrust ourselves to when it comes to those who teach God's Word. (And His justice for victims who have been purposefully led astray will not be thwarted.)

When we think in the context of Jesus's Sermon, what comes to mind are the religious leaders who kept the law of the Torah meticulously but whose hearts were far from God (Matt. 15:9). In this case, it wasn't so much that the Pharisees were teaching the wrong things; it's that they didn't *live* by what they were teaching and that they taught not to edify others but to be seen by them (Matt. 23:1–5). They were hypocrites, selfish, and burdened God's people with religious tradition. They appeared as sheep when in reality they were wolves, like thriving grape vines that were nothing but thorny bushes.

Thinking in terms of Pharisaic, Torah-keeping performance can feel removed from our culture, but Jesus's teaching is possibly even more relevant today than it was then. Because we now have global access to all manner of spiritual gurus, leaders, teachers, authors, and counselors, we must be vigilant to heed Jesus's words. We must measure a person's words against *the* Word. We must look for godliness over charisma, humility over celebrity status, servanthood over number of followers. One of the most sobering things Paul writes to young Timothy is that there will be charming and alluring people who will have a *form* of godliness but without the power that results from a true relationship with God (2 Tim. 3:5).

The point is not to turn us into judgment factories or send us on full-time witch hunts—this obsessive preoccupation equally has a "form of godliness" without a fiber of Christ's love, wisdom, or gentleness. Instead, we're to be discerning, prayerful, watchful, and patient. We must look for the good fruit of humility, kindness, gentleness, compassion, patience, quiet service, generosity, and a commitment to prayer. We may not be able to tell a sheep from a wolf immediately, but we at least need to know what we're looking for: people who are both inward *and* outward followers of Christ.

Lord, we want to bear fruit in keeping with repentance (Matt. 3:8). Before we think about the integrity of others, we ourselves want to be pure before You. Give us discernment so we are not deceived, patience so we don't jump to conclusions. Protect us from wolves in sheep's clothing, and make us forever and always good trees that bear good fruit in Your kingdom, for Your glory alone.

DAY 56

DOING GOD'S WILL

"Not everyone who says to me 'Lord, Lord,' will enter the kingdom of heaven, but only the one who does the will of my Father in heaven. On that day many will say to me, 'Lord, Lord, didn't we prophesy in your name, drive out demons in your name, and do many miracles in your name?' Then I will announce to them, 'I never knew you. Depart from me, you lawbreakers.'"

Matthew 7:21–23

My favorite Amazonian jungle guide took me and some of my friends on a tour through the renowned opera house in Manaus, Brazil. It was constructed during the rubber boom with many of the materials coming from Europe. To attend the theater there is to take your seat in Paris while living in the jungle. Milton led us to the prestigious balcony box seats that in the early 1900s were auctioned to the highest bidder. When we entered the private chamber, we realized these were the worst seats in the house. Only a small portion of the stage is visible from their position, but the people who sat in those seats were visible to the audience. Milton smiled widely at our perplexity, "These wealthy ticket holders," he explained, "did not come to *see* but to *be seen*."

This desire for notoriety while missing the "main show" may be part of what is behind today's passage. I spent many years as a child terrified of verses 13–23, again, mostly because I read them apart from the Sermon's context but also because they're just plain frightening—a serious warning that using our gifts in the name of Jesus doesn't necessarily mean He knows us. I never want to shield anyone from the Holy Spirit's conviction that rescues from the Broad Road to the Life Road.

But I do want to shield from needless terror those who earnestly love and seek after Christ. One of my favorite commentators assures us that today's passage "is not given to cause morbid introspection or undue self-doubt for the believer but rather to exhort one not to be enamored with external gifts and powers and behaviors without paying attention to the soul and heart."[80] And so let us move forward in hope as we ponder Christ's words.

In Jesus's day people were prophesying, casting out demons, and even performing miracles in His name, but they weren't doing His will (7:21). They were operating from the balcony seats to be seen, unwilling to see who Jesus is or to use their gifts for His glory. Notice, as well, that the miraculous acts these people were performing are all external activities—flashy displays that tend to draw a crowd, attract personal glory, and bring in money (Acts 8:18). It's interesting that so far in Jesus's Sermon, none of these external acts has been highlighted as a go-to characteristic of believers. Jesus has instead focused on acts of compassion; being salt and light through deliberate displays of mercy, humility, and purity; forgiving others; praying for those who wound us; being generous; not unfairly judging. In other words, the stuff that typically happens from the ground-floor level, often in obscurity, but always with a full view of Jesus.

So the warning He brings us is that if we're all about the religious acts that look sensational to everyone on the surface, but our inward lives, our private lives, our moral lives, don't align with God's kingdom and His righteousness, we may not know Him. If this is an accurate description of your life, then today is a day of repentance for you. Repentance is a wonderful gift because when we turn from our sin of self-reliance and doing religious things for applause, we turn to a kind and gentle Savior eager to forgive and receive us (Matt. 11:28–30).

For the genuine Christ follower, what a reminder this is of the premium Jesus places on *doing the will of our Father in heaven*. I have underlined verse 21 in my Bible because this is at the heart of Jesus's invitation: to obey Him. To do what He says to do, to be who He calls us to be. This may not always entail grandiose acts that attract a following, but nothing is more precious to God than doing His will, than plain obedience.

I've known a few people in my life who have suffered through cancer with a graciousness and joy I find more remarkable than if any of them could cast out demons. A family in my church who lost their daughter to a drunk driver walked the agonizing road of forgiving the man who took from them their beloved child. Every time I'm around this couple, I find their life more awe-inspiring than if they turned water into wine at my dinner table. I have dear friends who just received an entire family of refugees into their small home, and I'm more astounded than if they shared with me a word of prophecy. It's not that the more dramatic gifts are of no value or unimportant. It's that obedience to Jesus will always be more profound than grand religious acts, even ones that seem to be "working," because a transformed heart is the greatest miracle of all.

Are you coasting on grand acts or spiritual gifts while ignoring something Jesus has plainly asked of you? Are you more committed to noticeable religious displays than doing His will in situations where people won't see it?

May we live our lives not to be seen but to see Jesus as we do the will of our Father in heaven. As it turns out, this is to live from the best seats in the house.

DAY 57

OF ROCK AND SAND

"Therefore, everyone who hears these words of mine and acts on them will be like a wise man who built his house on the rock. The rain fell, the rivers rose, and the winds blew and pounded that house. Yet it didn't collapse, because its foundation was on the rock. But everyone who hears these words of mine and doesn't act on them will be like a foolish man who built his house on the sand. The rain fell, the rivers rose, the winds blew and pounded that house, and it collapsed. It collapsed with a great crash."

Matthew 7:24–27

Barbara Kingsolver's memoir, *Animal, Vegetable, Miracle,* details her family's year of living mostly from whatever their family farm yielded. When she wrote about the hard labor, particularly of chicken farming, she said, "Believing in the righteousness of a piece of work, alas, is not what gets it done."[81] She then went on to reminisce about the tiring efforts of lighting fires for warm kettles, sharpening knives for harvesting fowls. Her point is that believing in healthy, local food is only half the battle; lacing up your work boots and pulling weeds is what accomplishes your goal.

Jesus speaks to this same principle; only instead of addressing what's in the best interest of our bodies, He looks to the interest of our souls. At the end of His Sermon, He puts before us a straightforward question: What will you *do* with "these words of mine"? Will you be a hearer only or one who actually puts them into practice? This is the question His Sermon comes down to. It's the question that separates true disciples from all others. And today, we each have a fresh chance to be a wise follower, to build our lives on the solid rock of obedience.

The parable Jesus tells to illustrate this is just perfect because we can all understand things like solid houses versus dilapidated ones in the midst of bad weather. As I write, I'm adding a bedroom and screened porch to my 1930s home. So far I've had rain in my living room, a burst pipe in my basement, and a raccoon in my attic. Praise God, the house is still standing, given its sturdy foundation. That said, I am incalculably more interested in window treatments and bathroom tile selections than I am concrete footings. But, alas, when come the tornadoes, floods, and derechos, it will be the solid foundation, not the polished nickel fixtures, that will secure my shelter. I will huddle in the basement—as I have many times before—praying my builders built well versus built beautifully. And that I don't run into the raccoon.

The peculiar thing about the wise person's house and the foolish person's is that you can't tell whose is most solid from the outside. In Jesus's day, it is possible that from the street, metaphorically speaking, the Pharisee's home or the miracle worker's mansion were more magazine worthy than the modest house of the true disciple. The hypocrite may have had the front porch you've always wanted. It isn't until torrential weather rolls in that a person's foundations are revealed—sand or rock. Here we get to Jesus's point. Those who build their lives on sand are ones who have heard Jesus but who haven't obeyed Him. They haven't *acted* on what He said. But those whose lives are able to withstand the floods of tragedy, the rainfall of hardship, ultimately, the judgment day of Christ, are those who hear *and* act according to His words.

The Greek word for *act* is a word Jesus has already used a number of times in His Sermon. It emphasizes our need to put into practice what He teaches (Matt. 5:19; 6:1; 7:12).[82] A true disciple, one with "greater righteousness" is a person who is earnest about doing the will of the Father now understood through the teachings of Christ.[83] It's not enough to fall back on Bible knowledge without obeying what it says. Mentally assenting to the righteousness of something is "not what gets it done." Said another way, a life lived according to your beliefs proves what your beliefs are.

Dear reader, I want your house to be secure because you're doing what Jesus says. When fearsome winds come howling, when heartbreaking waves come crashing, when you stand before Jesus on the last day, there's no need for your life to blow apart. It is God's will that your life be found firmly on Christ who is your Rock (1 Cor. 10:4)! Being a believer in Jesus's gift of salvation results in being a doer of His teaching. This is the wise life, the house built on solid ground, the one that will endure because its foundation is on Him.

Do you believe in the things He's taught you? Then go walk in them.

DAY 58

A TEACHER LIKE NO OTHER

"When Jesus had finished saying these things, the crowds were astonished at his teaching, because he was teaching them like one who had authority, and not like their scribes."

Matthew 7:28–29

THIS HAS LONG BEEN ONE of my favorite passages because it reminds me of something we may have either forgotten or stopped believing: Jesus isn't boring. Sermons can occasionally be dull. Religion can get crusty. Messages can fall flat—I have given a few myself where suddenly people needed to "slip out." But no one was leaving or falling asleep the day Jesus taught by the Sea of Galilee. Referencing the astonished reaction of the crowds, Dietrich Bonhoeffer asks, "What had happened?" He answers himself, "The Son of God had spoken."[84] That's what happened.

The one who gave the message is the One who makes all the difference. It is not merely that the Sermon on the Mount is sound wisdom for those of us trying to navigate this crazy world. It's not that we've all finally figured out that forgiveness is good for a person's health, and generous people tend to be happier, and worry-free people sleep better so Jesus must have been on to something. It's not that Jesus was merely a sage, an insightful prophet, a unique rabbi, someone who would have made an interesting professor. He is God's Son, the radiance of God's glory, the exact representation of His being (Heb. 1:3), the One through whom all things were created (Col. 1:16). He is the fulfillment of the law and the prophets (Matt. 5:17). In Him all things hold together (Col. 1:17). He is King of kings and Lord of lords (1 Tim. 6:15)!

This is the man who is giving the Sermon, and when God's Son speaks truth about God's nature and how we can best flourish in our world, everyone leans in.

The crowds were bowled over by Him, absolutely astonished by what He taught and the authority He taught with because it all felt so different from their experience with the scribes. The scribes had an important task; it just wasn't an inventive one. They made judgments on the law based on interpretations rooted in earlier traditions.[85] They were careful protectors of the law, but they weren't the creators of it. In short, their job was to handle the law, not to *give* it. By contrast, Jesus shockingly revealed Himself to be the ultimate and final giver and interpreter of the law. The new standard of true righteousness was not found in keeping past religious traditions but in how a person responded to *His words*.[86]

So we must ask ourselves, who do we believe uttered these words? This is the question the Sermon on the Mount compels us to ask in the first place.[87] If it is Jesus, God's Son, then He can speak with nothing less than the authority of God. And if His teaching is life, if what He says is so compelling that the sick, the demon possessed, the paralyzed, the poor, the Jews, and the religious outsiders could only respond with, *Wow! We've never heard that before!*, how are we responding?

His words are as astonishing now as they were then. No teachings have proven more transcendent. I am too fearful to imagine the life I would be living had they not been hidden in my heart. When middle-school insecurity plagued me, I learned that I was fearfully and wonderfully made. When I was crushed and disappointed in my career, I read of God's sovereignty. Through mental and emotional turmoil, the Psalms comforted me and the epistles sustained me. Jesus's teachings have held and led me through loss and rejection, joy and celebration. My prayer is that this daily devotional through Jesus's longest recorded sermon has made you yearn for more. My hope is that you will commit yourself to the study of His Word that we all might be astonished together.

Because it's true—we really don't live by bread alone but by every word He speaks.

Creator God, if our hearts have cooled to Your Word, melt us with Your loving truth, astound us with Your wisdom, jolt us awake with Your inspiring call! Let us be nothing less than astonished. And on the days when nothing leaps off the pages of Scripture at us, may we delight in putting Your words into practice.

DAY 59

THE NEW AND GREATER MOSES

When he came down from the mountain, large crowds followed him.

Matthew 8:1

Do you remember what Jesus did when He first saw the crowds in Matthew 5:1? He ascended a mountain. It's been a little while, so you may not remember climbing up behind Him and finding your place in the grass. We have listened to His entire Sermon on the Mount, and now that his Sermon is over, we see Jesus descending that mount.

This is not a random detail. It would have stood out to the ancient reader. Jesus having taught His followers how to live and thrive in this world from a hillside in Galilee closely parallels the account of Moses coming down from Mount Sinai holding the Ten Commandments—the law that would teach Israel how best to live. Scholars throughout the centuries have seen this verse depicting Jesus as the new Moses. Moses was God's appointed lawgiver and Israel's great deliverer so this is no small assessment. But all along Moses was foreshadowing Jesus, our ultimate Deliverer, one who did not come to replace Moses's law but proved to be its fulfillment and the only one who could interpret it for us wholly and truly.[88] And as one insightful commentator explains, when Jesus descends the mountain, "he carries no tablets because he *is* the law."[89] All the righteousness and goodness of the law, all that men and women for centuries had been toiling to live up to, Jesus embodies.

Isn't this just an astounding thought?

And the parallels continue. The first time Moses descended Mount Sinai with the Ten Commandments (because remember there were two of these episodes), he walked straight into a show of debauchery that would make Las Vegas blush. The Israelites whom God had miraculously delivered from Egypt—in their recent past I might add—decided that Moses had left them too long in the wilderness and they needed some new gods to get them going again. According to Aaron, Moses's right-hand man, the people threw their gold jewelry into a fire and, lo and behold, out came a golden calf. What else could they do but worship it? When Moses saw the people dancing around the lifeless idol, he threw down the stone tablets, smashing them at the base of the mountain.

Jesus does not descend into the same kind of chaos as Moses, though we will soon find He descends into profound brokenness. And as we've already noted, He doesn't carry a physical law because He is the embodiment of all the goodness and truth God poured out to His people through Moses. No more tablets are broken, but Jesus will, "like the first tablets of the law, be broken by the disobedience of those he has come to save. . . . That he will be broken on the cross remains for many the reason they cannot see how Jesus can be the Son of God."[90]

I pray that you will freshly see Jesus as God's Son. I pray that if you've fallen back under the wearying "written code" of religiosity, those exacting "letters chiseled on stones," you will receive His body broken for you, His blood shed for you. Even if you're not well acquainted with Moses's life or the Ten Commandments, chances are you have certain standards you can't seem to meet, ones for which you keep striving, failing, and feeling guilty. I know this cycle well as a pastor's daughter, firstborn, graduate-level legalist. But the law of Jesus—though in a sense more demanding than Moses because He wants every part of us—is not burdensome because the Lawgiver and Life Giver Himself shares with us the load of all the carrying and doing. He is gentle and lowly in heart and invites you and me to come to Him (Matt. 11:28–30).

We will soon move on to the healings and miracles of Jesus. We'll encounter His love and compassion shown to both Jews and Gentiles, elite and outcast, young and old. But before we get to these remarkable encounters, where Jesus's teachings flow into compassionate actions, we must pause and consider His "coming down from the mountain."

He will come down to be broken. And in so doing, He will prove to be the one that Moses and his law had been pointing to all along. The one who would save His people from their sins.

PART 2
THE MIRACLES OF JESUS

At the beginning of this devotional, we looked at Matthew's literary organization and the way verses 4:23 and 9:35 form an *inclusio* around the teaching and healing portions of Jesus's ministry. Chapters 5–7 cover His ministry through teaching, and then chapters 8–9 subsequently explore His ministry through healings and miracles.

After Jesus's astonishing Sermon, we're about to stand up and stretch our legs. We'll follow Him down the hillside, amid the crowds and disciples, straight onto the pavement of sickness, need, fear, shame, or in other words: real life. Through ten encounters with all types of people, many on the fringes of society, we will have the privilege of seeing Jesus live the Sermon He just preached. And when we get to the end of chapter 9, we'll realize He has asked us to go and live it too.

DAY 60

TO BE MADE CLEAN

Right away a man with leprosy came up and knelt before him, saying, "Lord, if you are willing, you can make me clean."

Matthew 8:2

I HOPE I WILL NEVER get over Matthew's careful packaging of Jesus's teachings and miracles. He thoughtfully folded tender stories of Jesus's compassionate encounters with people (Matt. 8–9) into the dough of His teachings (Matt. 5–7), or maybe the other way around. Jesus's good teaching and good actions are inseparable. Both His words and touch heal.

As soon as Jesus comes down the mountain where He had spoken to a people who needed His words, a leper approaches Him in need of His touch. But as we know from contagious diseases, needing a touch is problematic. Even in our own day we would rather not come into contact with someone who has poison ivy or cuddle a child with the flu. Once when my niece Harper was five, she spent the night at my house and woke me up around midnight, faintly moaning about needing to throw up. It's really too bad the whole event couldn't have been officially clocked because I moved at world-record speed to get her off my white, natural fiber carpet and into the bathroom. *How do parents do this all the time?* I mused. And then I wondered how I would physically console her without getting sick myself. Because we know how this goes: the sick contaminate the healthy, not the other way around.

In ancient Jewish culture having leprosy meant bearing an added stigma worse than the disease itself. Practicing Jews were aware of the laws about skin diseases written in Leviticus 13–14. Leprosy not only rendered a person physically unclean but ceremonially so. The disease cut a person off from their family, their community, and life in the temple. The isolation and shame were unbearable. In Old Testament times a leper venturing out into public would have to call out, "Unclean, unclean!" so everyone knew to stay away.

This was the life of the man who fell on His knees before Jesus.

He begins by calling Jesus "Lord," a term of divinity that gives insight into who the leper may have understood Jesus to be. (At the very least the leper saw Him as powerful and kind.) It's a term we must grapple with today. Is Jesus Lord? Is He worthy of our kneeling before Him in adoration, yes, even desperation?

The suffering man continues, "If you are willing, you can make me clean." His words are full of faith and humility. He doesn't place demands on Jesus but affirms His healing capabilities. To this man, it's not a matter of Jesus's power; it's a matter of His willingness. I wonder if Matthew didn't have in mind the asking, seeking, and knocking Jesus had just encouraged when he wrote about this leper. The ailing man doesn't come *claiming* his healing, only asking for it as would a child for a piece of bread or a freshly filleted fish. But he does come *believing* in the authority and tenderness of Christ.

We might expect the leper to ask to be healed or to be made well, but he asks to be made clean. This was how cured lepers were always described in the New Testament—not healed but *cleansed* (Matt. 10:8; 11:5). Once again this highlights the man's reality—he wasn't merely sick; he was ceremonially unclean, cut off from religious life. The latter was his true trauma. For Jesus to heal him was for Jesus to cleanse him.

Perhaps you too need to be cleansed. Maybe you need a fresh portion of God's forgiveness. Possibly you're crumbling underneath shame that only Christ can lift from your soul. Shame no one else can see but you can nonetheless feel every day. What would restoration look like? Perhaps it would mean reconciled relationships, or once again walking in the light as Christ is in the light. Come to Him for healing. In the words of Jesus's beloved disciple, "If we confess our sins, he is faithful and righteous to forgive us our sins and to *cleanse* us from all unrighteousness (1 John 1:9).

He is not only able to do this for you; He is willing.

DAY 61

TO NOT BE ALONE

Reaching out his hand, Jesus touched him, saying, "I am willing; be made clean." Immediately his leprosy was cleansed. Then Jesus told him, "See that you don't tell anyone; but go, show yourself to the priest, and offer the gift that Moses commanded, as a testimony to them."

Matthew 8:3–4

THERE'S SOMETHING ABOUT THE INCARNATION of Christ that goes beyond its theological necessity. True, we cannot be saved apart from God in the flesh, but it's also likely true that we cannot know how loved we are. God without a body, God without fingers and nerve endings and callouses could not press His skin against the skin of a leper. "Jesus *touched* him." God certainly healed people in the Old Testament in various ways, but only God in human form, only Jesus, can offer the sort of touch the leper received. The sort of human connection that says, *You are not alone.*

The leper's body must have jolted to life at the mere sensation of physical contact. What must it have been like to have not been touched for as long as he'd had the disease, to see Jesus's hand move toward him unafraid, to feel someone else's skin against his own? The man was immediately cleansed of his leprosy, but what else was healed? Wounds of rejection and isolation, I imagine. The emotional toll must have begun to lift as Jesus's touch sent stigmas flying.

No one had dared get close to this man; now Jesus had declared him clean.

It's shocking how much is contained in this tiny scene. Did Jesus defile Himself by becoming ceremonially unclean when He touched the leper? How is it that instead of the unclean defiling the clean, which is how this world works, Jesus's cleanness overcame the leper's disease? And what do we make of Jesus's seeming violation of Old Testament law (Lev. 5:3) by touching a leper? Perhaps most of our technical questions are settled by this one phrase that Jesus loved to quote from the prophet Hosea: "I desire mercy, not sacrifice" (Matt. 9:13). By disregarding social and religious taboos, Jesus showed that to fulfill the law is to do the very things for which it was intended: love your neighbor as yourself. Move toward them and invite them into the fellowship of believers.

The leper was now not only physically clean but had the opportunity to become ceremonially so. Since the sacrificial laws of the religious system remained in place for the Jews until Jesus's death and resurrection, Jesus encouraged this man to go to the temple, offer his gift, and show himself to the priest as a *testimony*.[91]

What testimony do you have? From what has Jesus cleansed you, healed you, freed you? What fellowship of believers has He brought you into? He is most certainly still in the business of working miracles. Don't hold back your praise, beloved, for "those in desperate need cannot afford to rationalize away God's power and compassion."[92] I've been agonizingly desperate before. Perhaps you have too. Jesus meets us uniquely in those conditions, sometimes bringing immediate relief, other times asking us to walk out a process—even the freshly cleansed leper still had some things to take care of in the temple.

Dear friend, Jesus's power and compassion did not evaporate after His resurrection. He is present with us now through His Holy Spirit. He is no less able to touch, heal, raise to life, mend, or cleanse. His compassion still tears through our prejudices and religious snobbery. This of course does not mean Jesus *must* do what we ask; His yeses and nos can remain a mystery even while we trust that He is altogether good and present with us, promising never to forsake His own.

Perhaps my favorite part of this short account is thinking about this man waltzing into the temple, chin up, carrying his gift in his unstained arms, seeing people for the first time, "Hey Fred, it's been a while!" This is a story about many things, but not the least of which it's a story about not being alone anymore.

DAY 62

HIS POWER AND COMPASSION

When he entered Capernaum, a centurion came to him, pleading with him, "Lord, my servant is lying at home paralyzed, in terrible agony."

He said to him, "Am I to come and heal him?"

"Lord," the centurion replied, "I am not worthy to have you come under my roof. But just say the word, and my servant will be healed. For I too am a man under authority, having soldiers under my command. I say to this one, 'Go,' and he goes; and to another, 'Come,' and he comes; and to my servant, 'Do this!' and he does it."

Matthew 8:5–9

I AM MOVED BY JESUS'S passion for the nations. His heartbeat for every tribe, tongue, and skin color resonates in my core. I'm all about His care for the misfit, foreigner, and vulnerable, perhaps because I myself have felt on the outside at times. I will cheer all day for the way He loves all manner of people. That is, until I'm confronted with having to love a person (or group of people) I don't like. Then I'm superannoyed by the whole thing. I fear I am not alone here.

For the Jews in Jesus's day, a centurion would have landed squarely in the category of people not to like. As a Gentile, this centurion was not only considered unclean to the Jew but was a symbol of Roman oppression. How could a Jew living in the land of Israel be expected to have any warm thoughts whatsoever toward a person outside of God's covenant people, a captain of a legion of troops occupying Israel's sacred land? Surely Jesus could in good conscience kindly refuse to help him, signaling to His disciples that they too were off the hook. But, then again, there was that part in Jesus's Sermon about going the extra mile, turning the other cheek, not just tolerating one's enemies but praying for and loving them. Apparently, Jesus meant for His teachings to be acted upon, not just listened to. Lest we forget about the sand and rock.

The leper was a religious outsider, the centurion an ethnic outsider, yet both called Jesus "Lord." We don't know how much either person understood of Jesus's full divinity, but both approached Him respectfully, believing in His power and kindness. The centurion also had a special understanding of Jesus's authority. We don't much like this word today, but good and just authority is essential to our sense of order, peace, and well-being. Just as the centurion could command his officers to do something and they would do it, he believed illness and death were under Jesus's authority. Yet the centurion was considerate of the great Jew-Gentile divide. He knew that for Jesus to even come under his roof to heal his servant would make Him ceremonially unclean, so he had an idea for Jesus: "Just say the word." The centurion believed it to be the only thing needed for his servant to be healed.

You have to wonder how this many-times-over outsider had the eyes to see the miracle-working power of Jesus that so many of the insiders seemed to be missing. For Jesus to merely speak a word from a distance and heal the centurion's servant is not the stuff of sages, scribes, or prophets; it's the stuff of God. But it's not only that the centurion believed in Jesus's divine power to heal. The astounding part is "that he, a Gentile, believed that the compassion and healing of Jesus could reach across the divide between Jew and Gentile and touch a Gentile's servant."[93] In other words, it wasn't just the power of God that the centurion saw in Jesus; it was the compassion of God.

Here's the thing: believing in Jesus's power is essential to our faith, but believing in His compassion is what changes our hearts. To know that He is kind enough, loving enough, moved enough to reach all the way to your forbidden places, to cross the tracks, to give His life for you "while we were still sinners" (Rom. 5:8), is what sets Jesus apart from all others. It is necessary that you believe in His power. But do you also believe in His compassion *for you*? Ask Him for the faith to believe it, and you will find yourself in the company of the centurion, who saw what even the insiders missed because he dared to believe that Jesus is just that good.

DAY 63

A PLACE AT THE BANQUET

Hearing this, Jesus was amazed and said to those following him, "Truly I tell you, I have not found anyone in Israel with so great a faith. I tell you that many will come from east and west to share the banquet with Abraham, Isaac, and Jacob in the kingdom of heaven. But the sons of the kingdom will be thrown into the outer darkness where there will be weeping and gnashing of teeth." Then Jesus told the centurion, "Go. As you have believed, let it be done for you." And his servant was healed that very moment.

Matthew 8:10–13

I HAD A WISE COUNSELOR who helped me a great deal in my twenties and early thirties. Barbara was the type of person who was always for you even when she had to shoot straight with you. She never shied away from prescribing the Bible truth even if the Bible truth meant a whole bunch of things in your life might explode and land in inconvenient places. She entrusted herself and those she counseled to the living God. Her faith in Him made you want to trust Him too.

Many years after counseling with Barbara, I ran into her daughter at a party. I asked her how her mom was doing, and in the course of conversation she said, "My mom has a very big God." I haven't stopped thinking about this. A person doesn't make God small or big; He is. But I knew what her daughter meant. Barbara believes God to be all He says He is: very big, indeed. This faith rubbed off on those she counseled.

For the centurion's part, He too had a very big Jesus. He believed Him to be more powerful, more authoritative, more compassionate than the people of Israel, the ones who were supposed to "get it." Matthew tells us that Jesus was *amazed* at this Gentile outsider's faith, which is significant because Jesus is only "amazed" one other time in the Gospels. In Mark 6:6, He is amazed at the Jews' *lack* of faith. So we ask ourselves: Is Jesus amazed at our faith in Him—even when circumstances are bleak and trying—or is He astounded at how small we've made Him to be?

In the middle of His dialogue with the centurion, Jesus turns to His own people and gives a mini-teaching. The ones invited to Abraham, Isaac, and Jacob's future banquet will be people of faith in Jesus. Being a physical descendant of Abraham won't be enough. In other words, insiders who look solely to their Israelite heritage and depend on their outward religious activity will be cast out. But outsiders like the Gentile centurion whose faith is in Jesus will have a place at the table.

What an opportunity we have to follow Jesus now and one day sit at His table forever! It will be a lavish celebration where we will feast and rejoice with all those who know they don't belong there on their own merit and as a result are all the more grateful to be there. Conversely, Jesus's short statement is also a warning to those who assume they're "in" because they come from godly parents, or have religious friends, or are affiliated with a church, or are pretty good people yet do not actually know Him. This need not be our fate. We can have faith as did the centurion. We can call Jesus our "Lord" and believe Him for God-sized things because God is who He is.

Jesus turns back to the centurion and simply says, "Go." The centurion was free to return to his servant because, as Jesus immediately makes known, his servant is now healed. Jesus is demonstrating what He's just explained—that whoever submits to Him as Lord, Jew or Gentile, will find healing and a place at His table.

Jesus's ability to heal with a word brings us back to His healing of the leper. That Jesus touched the man's diseased skin suddenly takes on a deeper meaning because now we understand that Jesus didn't have to touch him. He could have spared His reputation, could have stuck with the law of not defiling Himself, not becoming ceremonially unclean. A word instead of a touch would have at the very least made things a lot less gruesome and uncomfortable. But the leper needed more than physical healing; he needed to know that even when he was sick and repulsive to everyone else, he was lovable to Christ. He was valued, body and soul.

Yes, we have a very big God indeed.

DAY 64

A WOMAN'S HEALING AND CALLING

Jesus went into Peter's house and saw his mother-in-law lying in bed with a fever. So he touched her hand, and the fever left her. Then she got up and began to serve him.

Matthew 8:14–15

THIS IS THE THIRD AND shortest account of the first three healings that Matthew threads together for us. After compassionately touching a leper and astounding His followers by healing a Gentile's servant, Jesus travels to tend to Peter's mother in-law. When Jesus entered Peter's house, Luke's Gospel tells us He rebuked the woman's fever. Luke's strong language implies that perhaps an evil spirit lay behind her illness. No matter the cause, she was healed the moment Jesus laid His hand on her own.

Here again we encounter both the power and compassion of Jesus. Just a word would have done it, but how much more tender His touch? Not to mention a word of healing may have been less controversial given that a rabbi touching a woman's hand went against at least some Jewish traditions of the day.[94] But Jesus never adhered to man-made traditions that stood in the way of His mission of loving people. If she needed His touch, the people could think what they may. And this is not to mention that Jesus did all this on the Sabbath. How He loved to upend the parts of the religious system that were unhinged from God's heart.

So while it seems normal to our modern sensibilities that Jesus would enter Peter's home to heal his mother in-law, His determined care for her was especially tender, if not uncustomary. Women did not hold a prominent place in society in ancient Judaism, something Jesus often made a point of confronting. He would continue to barrel through taboos to heal women, esteem them, and fold them into special places of His ministry. The arrival of His kingdom meant a new day for women, one that's still lighting the way.

Jesus deems this suffering woman as worthy of not only His healing touch but also His call. As soon as He touched her, she sat up and began to serve Him. (Mark and Luke include that she served the other disciples as well.) The Greek word translated as "serve" here is a word the New Testament epistles often use to describe Christian discipleship. Some scholars suggest that this woman's serving isn't just about being able to resume activities like getting the teakettle going or assembling the charcuterie board, but it may also describe the moment her discipleship to Christ began.[95] A new day, indeed. In other words, more than serving guests in her household, it may be the case that she began serving the mission of Christ and His fledgling people.

Regardless of the possible interpretations, the definitive part of this woman's story is that her healing did not result in her sitting up and then darting off to meaningless activities. She had good, kingdom work to do. Sometimes I wonder if this is why Jesus touched her hand and not her fever-stricken forehead, because He knows a woman's hands are uniquely scrappy and resourceful. What kingdom things a sold-out woman for Jesus can get done with her hands!

With her restored health and seasoned abilities, she did what I hope you and I will do with the healing we've received from Jesus: serve Him and others with everything we have.

From what has Jesus healed you? It may be from a physical illness, but it could also be from an emotional or psychological ailment. Maybe He's delivered you from a terrible relationship or pulled you out of a pit of your own making. Perhaps He rescued you during a time you couldn't even call out to Him. (It bears noting that when Peter's mother in-law was too ill to pursue Jesus, Jesus pursued her.) Whatever He has done for you, are you serving Him and others out of your healing? What wonderful work He has for you to do. Will you put your heart and hands to His good use? He hasn't just delivered you from things like sin, sickness, and brokenness; He has delivered you to Himself.

DAY 65

JESUS MAKES A WAY

Right away a man with leprosy came up and knelt before him. . . . When he entered Capernaum, a centurion came to him. . . . Jesus went to Peter's house and saw his mother in-law lying in bed with a fever.

Matthew 8:2, 5, 14

The accounts of the leper, the centurion, and Peter's mother in-law are meant to be digested together. If the leper was a religious outcast and the centurion an ethnic one, Peter's mother in-law would also have been considered somewhat of a second-class citizen within Judaism, given that she is a woman.[96] Up to this point, all three types of people were excluded from full participation in Israel's worship.[97] I will never get over what Matthew is depicting for us here. What might seem like a mere chronological list of healings is actually his handpicked selection of three categorically similar situations: suffering outsiders whom Jesus has ministered to and invited to become insiders. These three miracles foreshadow His coming for all people, His flinging wide the doors to His kingdom for any and all who might believe and follow Him.

Herod's temple gives us a literal picture of the hierarchies and separation that characterized Jewish life in Jesus's day. Lepers were confined to a reserved area near the temple; non-Jews could inch a little closer to the most holy place by entering the court of Gentiles; and women could get even closer while in the court of women. But none had access to the court of the Israelites, much less the holy of holies, which was reserved only for purified Jewish men.

By moving toward the leper, the centurion, and Peter's mother in-law, Jesus shows His power over sickness and disease and His compassion for those often dismissed by society, but He reveals something more: full access to God is not found in Torah observance or temple worship but only and fully in Him. Disease, race, gender, societal power, denominational affiliation neither qualifies nor disqualifies. The standard for entrance into the kingdom of heaven is met only in Christ. Belonging to Him is all that matters.

Each of these three healings was but a flickering light of the blast that was to come at Jesus's death and resurrection. As the author of Hebrews explains, Jesus entered the most holy place by His own blood, obtaining eternal redemption for us all (Heb. 9:11–12): Jew, Gentile, slave, free, male, female. Where the lepers couldn't go, where the Gentiles were held back, where the women were stopped short, Jesus went for them.

He went for *you.*

And where the high priests were continually limited by their sacrifices that could never take away sins, Jesus sacrificed Himself for all who will come to Him. He went where we couldn't go; He did what we couldn't do.

I have this memory from my late teens of coming home from church choir practice (I have just dated myself into the 1800s) and sitting in the sunroom of our family's home, reflecting. I was riddled with anxiety at the time. For some reason the confinement of that choir loft brought me both sensations of belonging and panic. It wasn't the people or anyone's lack of carrying a tune that caused the latter; it was what the holiness of church cast upon my young and sensitive soul. I worried about my sin. Beleaguered by guilt that sprang from both my own doings and others, I knew I didn't have what it took for that "greater righteousness."

On that Sunday afternoon I opened my Bible to Hebrews. When I got to the part about the blood of goats and calves never being able to take away our sins, the part where Jesus made us clean by His own blood, a flood of relief washed over me. I'd been walking with Jesus for many years by then, but the joy of my salvation was renewed. Perhaps today is a day of renewed joy for you. Sometimes it's only a matter of remembering how you were once on the outside, but because Jesus entered the perfect and heavenly tabernacle by means of His own blood, you are now on the inside. You are now freely and fully a citizen of His kingdom.

DAY 66

HE TOOK AND CARRIED

When evening came, they brought to him many who were demon-possessed. He drove out the spirits with a word and healed all who were sick, so that what was spoken through the prophet Isaiah might be fulfilled: He himself took our weaknesses and carried our diseases.

Matthew 8:16–17

Anyone who has suffered with long-term disease, illness, or oppression will understand the mass flocking to Jesus's side for instantaneous and total healing. We have swarmed to celebrities who were signing autographs at the mall for far less. Matthew says that with a *word* demons dispersed and *all* who were sick He made well. That the people came as soon as the sun had set on the Sabbath and normal activities could resume is not surprising. To be free, to be healed in a moment—who wouldn't have run to Jesus? What a gathering this must have been.

Jesus did these things "so that" one of Isaiah's prophecies might be fulfilled. Matthew quotes from Isaiah 53, a chapter precious to Christians who see Jesus as the Suffering Servant about whom Isaiah writes. The coming Messiah would suffer and know sickness. He would be pierced for our rebellion and crushed for our sins. Our punishment would literally be placed upon Him. As New Testament believers, we most often look at this passage as dealing with our atonement: Christ's substitutionary death on our behalf. Matthew, however, highlights a portion of the prophecy that speaks specifically to the Messiah's taking on our sickness and disease (Isa. 53:4).

For the longest time I either hopped clear over this verse or assumed that when Matthew said Jesus carried our diseases what he actually meant was that He carried our sin. Indeed, Jesus took our sin upon Himself. But where does physical healing come in? Perhaps more than any other theological dilemma, why God heals some and not others is at the top for me. We all know people who have suffered extensively and profoundly. You may be suffering yourself.

If you are, you're not alone. As I have been trying to write this day's devotional, my heart has been distracted by real-life battles with friends whose cancer has just returned unexpectedly, a loved one still in long-felt pain, an infant with a tumor. I sometimes weary in praying. I wonder when the "word" will come, when the touch will cast out or heal. Do my prayers affect the outcome? I imagine you too have had these questions, these doubts, these wearying circumstances. I know there are those who say that miracles were for a different time and that Jesus doesn't do those things anymore, but I don't believe it. I trust He is still healing and delivering and making well, though sometimes I wonder if it's easier to believe He never heals on earth than to accept He only does it sometimes.

When answers to age-old questions aren't fully satisfactory, we can take great comfort in the words "took" and "carried." Jesus took our weakness and carried our diseases, and these are words of sharing.[98] There is no suffering He Himself doesn't intimately know. There is no pain you are experiencing that He is not well acquainted with. He is with you in it. And you don't have to explain to Him what you're going through because somehow He has taken it upon Himself. Jesus's incarnation cannot be overstated: He took on our bodily form and carried our ailments, knowing them more intimately than we know them ourselves.

Dearest Jesus, today we pray for miracles, for physical healing, for deliverance from evil oppression. Like the leper, we don't demand it, but we humbly say, "If you are willing." Like the centurion we believe in your power—just a "word" will do it. And for those too sick to ask for themselves like Peter's mother in-law, we ask on their behalf. And we trust that whatever You choose not to heal on earth, You will heal in the end.[99] We thank You for being a God who shared in our suffering and has never, and will never, leave us alone.

DAY 67

AN OVEREAGER DISCIPLE

When Jesus saw a large crowd around him, he gave the order to go to the other side of the sea. A scribe approached him and said, "Teacher, I will follow you wherever you go."

Jesus told him, "Foxes have dens, and birds of the sky have nests, but the Son of Man has no place to lay his head."

Matthew 8:18–20

After three astounding miracles and a momentous gathering where Jesus healed all who'd come to Him, Matthew didn't want us to get the wrong idea about discipleship. Perhaps this is why he introduces us to two potential disciples (one overeager, one undereager) who seem confused about what discipleship to Christ actually requires.[100] The life of following Him isn't about bouncing from one miracle to the next, and it isn't a guarantee that our lives will go just as we've planned. Any Christ follower will attest. Yet so many phenomenal things happen on the road of discipleship, we literally wouldn't trade it for the world. But, boy, are there some unglamorous, unglorious seasons. Discipleship costs us something.

The first of the two aspiring disciples is a scribe, a dedicated teacher of the law who's ready to go anywhere Jesus is going. He addresses Jesus as "Teacher," meaning he is impressed with Him as a rabbi though probably doesn't consider Him Lord. (As one who struggled to relinquish the title "boss of myself," I eventually realized that "Jesus as Lord" is a pretty key principle of discipleship.) Perhaps this man had heard about the supernatural wonders Jesus had performed, or maybe he'd visited the synagogue and heard one of His astonishing sermons. All we know is he wanted in on the action.

The fervor of this would-be disciple reminds me of moments I had growing up in the church. By the fourth day of summer church camp, with all its shaving cream games and emotional sharing and ziplining, I was ready to follow Jesus anywhere that promised s'mores. I loved summer camp, but every year the same strange thing happened: I had to go back home, back to school, back to work. My obedience to Jesus would be proven in those places more than around the campfires.

Later in Matthew's Gospel, Jesus would teach a similar principle about the difference between the seed of His Word falling onto good soil and its landing on soil that was rocky or thorn infested. The good soil represents receptive and understanding hearts; the other surfaces depict shallow gospel reception. Rocks, thorns, and seed-stealing birds are all images of what happens when a person captures some joyful element of God's Word but has no deep or abiding Christ-root to sustain when times get tough. In other words, if following Jesus is only about what He can give us and never what it will cost us, it's likely His gospel hasn't truly made it into our hearts.

Can you imagine the overly zealous "disciple" getting on the road with Jesus and then realizing He and His followers don't have a lasting home on this earth? Or what if this man set out behind Jesus for another round of miracles only to find out persecution was part of the call? We don't know what ended up happening to this scribe, whether He ultimately followed Jesus or not. We can only answer for ourselves.

What is holding you back from following Jesus where He leads? This may mean forsaking some familiar comforts. It might occasionally mean disrupting your relationships when following Him leads you away from friends or loved ones who are heading in different directions. It means dying to your earthly desires and agendas for His. It means He is more than just a good teacher with helpful thoughts for your life; He is Lord of your life.

When Jesus told the scribe that following Him meant a life without a permanent earthly home, He wasn't delivering the bad news; He was simply delivering the whole story. If the scribe was set on following Him,

Jesus wanted the man to know all he was signing up for. We follow Jesus not because He gives us everything we want but because He's worth everything we have. Don't be fooled about what it takes to follow Christ—He has let you in on just how hard it might be. At the same time, don't let counting the cost of discipleship deter you. Let it prove how worthy He is of your life, your all.

DAY 68

AN UNDEREAGER DISCIPLE

"Lord," another of his disciples said, "first let me go bury my father."

But Jesus told him, "Follow me, and let the dead bury their own dead."

Matthew 8:21–22

Yesterday we looked at the overly zealous scribe ready to follow Jesus without realizing the cost of discipleship. Today we'll look at an undereager "disciple" who puts off commitment to Jesus because He doesn't understand the high calling of being His follower. I suppose if the overeager man hadn't counted the cost of discipleship, the undereager one hadn't calculated the worth of following Jesus. We can err on both sides. It is true that the feel-good moments of our faith aren't what ultimately sustain us, but it's also true that falling in love with Jesus means we won't want to hold off becoming His disciple. When we get it, we go.

I remember thinking as a kid that I didn't want the Lord to come back before I'd taken a certain vacation, or performed at some incredible venue, or gotten married (I am just now realizing *I* might be responsible for delaying His return). But this of course is to not grasp the utter glory, joy, and riches of His coming back. This undereager "disciple" (a loose term here) similarly didn't grasp the worth and privilege of what it meant to be an earthly follower of Christ. Yet who could fault him? He wanted to be able to bury his father. Surely Jesus would understand this.

In ancient Judaism, a burial took place immediately following a person's death so it's unlikely this man was out talking with Jesus after having just lost his father. It's possible he was asking for time to "rebury" his father, a ritual that sometimes happened a year after the first burial.[101] It's even more likely the disciple's father was still living and the son was simply requesting to put off discipleship to Jesus until after his father had passed away and he'd had a chance to bury him and handle the necessary family matters, something that could have taken years.[102] What's more, he may have been waiting to shore up his inheritance before setting out to be a disciple.[103] We can trust Jesus was not being insensitive to a grieving man who had just lost his dad. We can also admit Jesus's words still cause us to wince if we're really listening. Allegiance to Him over people is still necessary.

I remember when I first became acutely aware of the fact that I had made people into idols. These certain individuals had become false gods not because I thought they could do the kind of supernatural things only God can do but because I'd given them ultimate priority in my heart. Their approval of me kept me going; their disapproval left me reeling. After many painful years of working through this with the Lord (idolatry still surfaces for me), it eventually occurred to me that I can love others the most when I'm loving Christ the best.

It's not that this would-be disciple's father wasn't important; it's that Jesus is infinitely more so. And when Jesus has His rightful place in our hearts, others will too. It's a funny thing that when no one in your life is more important than Jesus, everyone in your life becomes more important. It's about priorities. When Jesus is at the top, everyone else's status in our heart is lifted, yet not idolized, because He tells us to love others as we love ourselves.

When Jesus said, "Let the dead bury their dead," it seems to me He was communicating that temporal people will be about temporal things. Let them be. But those who have heard the call, "Follow Me," will not want to put off discipleship to Jesus for a single moment. We will not want to miss being an alive person who's about alive and eternal things.

Lord, don't let anything stand in the way of our following You today. We confess any human allegiance that would cause us to put off being Your disciple. We want to love You most, and by doing so we will love others best.

DAY 69

FOLLOW ME

As he got into the boat, his disciples followed him. Suddenly, a violent storm arose on the sea, so that the boat was being swamped by the waves—but Jesus kept sleeping.

Matthew 8:23–24

I once heard a friend teach on this passage. After reading these verses, she distinguished between the would-be disciples and Jesus's true followers, and what a word it was: she explained that the ones who have fully said "yes" to Jesus are the ones in the boat with Him.[104] The overly zealous scribe and the procrastinating would-be disciple had not fully said yes, for they were not in the boat. Followers such as Peter, Andrew, James, and John, His true disciples, were in there, and contrary to all my Christian sensibilities, being in the boat with Jesus did not ensure smooth sailing. They literally followed Him into a storm.

One afternoon overlooking the Amazon River, I sat with my Brazilian missionary friend, Darcy. A woman in her mid-sixties, she'd grown up in a sophisticated city in southern Brazil, a world away from the vast jungles of the rain forest. We sat on a meager wooden bench, peering out over the river, surrounded by humidity that laughs in the face of hair product. Darcy told me that more than forty years prior she and her husband Gioval followed God's call to live as missionaries in the Amazon. She didn't want to do it. With the straightest expression you've ever seen, she explained how much she hated water, boats, snakes, mosquitos, and heat. I so wished for her sake we'd been overlooking the French Riviera. For a time, it seemed that Darcy had followed Jesus to the wrong place—that she had gotten into the wrong boat.

After years of service in a large Amazonian city, Jesus prompted Darcy and Gioval to go even deeper into the jungle, to get to those most everyone else had forgotten about. Darcy initially resisted. Depression settled into her soul until obedience finally gave way to a newfound joy. After several days on the river, they arrived at their destination, a humble village brimming with largely forgotten, beautiful people.

Disembarking riverboats in the Amazon usually means a tenuous walk down a bouncy wooden plank that serves as a crude overpass between boat and land. I have walked them many times and never once elegantly. Darcy recalled the narrow plank that stood between her and the countless children, the tired moms and somber dads who desperately needed hope. She was afraid, plucked from her normal environment, and feeling ill-equipped. For Darcy, following Jesus literally meant "walking the plank."

She followed Him afraid, tenuously across the bouncing wooden slat. When her foot touched land, she recalled a flood of peace and joy washing over her. The glee on the children's faces, the hope in the eyes of parents needing tangible help and soul renewal attested to why Jesus had called her there. Her depression lifted. I had seen it for myself. Darcy's countenance testified of her transformation.

To be in the boat with Jesus is to have said yes to following Him. Each of our boats and planks will be different, but they're part of what it means to follow Him (a big theme of Matthew in this section). When we consider the overeager and undereager disciples on the shore with the disciples in the boat, we see that true discipleship isn't merited by personality or vocation, only by our response to Jesus.

Has someone or something kept you from saying yes to Him? This is the question we must ask ourselves. And if you find yourself in the middle of a storm as a result of following Him, don't wish to be with the fair weather "disciples" back on land. It's infinitely better to be in a storm with Jesus than in calm circumstances without Him.

"As he got into the boat, *his disciples followed him.*" May we follow Him too.

DAY 70

JESUS IS GOD

So the disciples came and woke him up, saying,
"Lord, save us! We're going to die!"

He said to them, "Why are you afraid, you of little faith?" Then he got up and rebuked the winds and the sea, and there was a great calm.

The men were amazed and asked, "What kind of man is this? Even the winds and the sea obey him!"

Matthew 8:25–27

This is a familiar story for many, even for those who didn't grow up in church. Partly because it's so accessible. Who can't relate to being tossed about in a raging storm, even if for most of us the storm is metaphorical. We're drawn to the idea of Jesus's rebuking whatever our storm is—disease, financial loss, strained relationships, wayward children. Perhaps in the middle of a personal trial someone has even said to you with great confidence, "Jesus can calm your storm!" This is not false, and the message of this story is not less than that, but it's much, much more.

The context helps explain this. Verses 1–17 reveal Jesus's power over *sickness and disease*; verses 23–27 reveal His power over *nature*. We'll soon see His power over *sin* (8:28–35; 9:4–7). It is Jesus's ultimate authority over *everything* Matthew continues to put on display here. There is nothing that won't submit to Him when He requires it. This was progressively becoming clearer to the disciples. They certainly didn't get it all at once, and we don't either. Much as our own faith develops in difficult times, we can watch their understanding of who He is grow during the storm.

It's not unreasonable to want out of storms, but there's a treasure to be had in them. How is God growing your faith in the middle of your trial? What are you learning about Him, about yourself?

Often in such storms Jesus shows His power not because of our great faith but to inspire in us a greater faith. How many times have we taken a step of obedience into the boat, only to find out halfway across the lake that we were in for a storm we hadn't signed up for, one we weren't sure Jesus was big enough to handle? But then we watched Him handle it (maybe over a length of time), and we realized He is more able, more God than we ever knew Him to be. Moreover, we couldn't even be smug about our grand amount of faith because we found out that, like the disciples, ours was only a "little." We came through the storm with a greater faith not because we had given Him so much to work with while in the boat but because He had shown Himself to be God.

That's what's going on in this account. The disciples were in a literal storm, which is important because when Jesus rebuked the wind and the waves, He was not only taking charge over nature; He was showing His God-ness. The Old Testament sheds light on this for us. The disciples in the boat would have been familiar with many passages about God's rule over the sea, but Psalm 89:8–9 stands out.

> *Lord God of Armies,*
> *who is strong like you, Lord?*
> *Your faithfulness surrounds you.*
> *You rule the raging sea;*
> *when its waves surge, you still them.*

The Jews understood that only Yahweh was capable of stilling storms. This authority and power belonged to God and God alone. So what should astound us about this story isn't only that Jesus had managed the disciples' personal predicament (even an extreme one); it's that He had revealed Himself as God in human flesh! The disciples were waking up to this reality. It's why they asked among themselves, "What kind of man is this?" because they very well knew: mere men can't do this kind of thing. Only God can.

This story is a matter of Christology (the nature of Jesus).

This famous moment in the Gospel of Matthew is an even better story than one that merely holds out what Jesus is capable of doing for us because it's a story about His divinity.[105] The disciples got into the boat with someone they viewed as rabbi or master and climbed out of the boat with someone they understood to be much closer to the Son of God.

And if Jesus is God, what can He not do for us when it's in His good will to do it?

DAY 71

ACROSS THE LAKE

When he had come to the other side, to the region of the Gadarenes, two demon-possessed men met him as they came out of the tombs. They were so violent that no one could pass that way. Suddenly they shouted, "What do you have to do with us, Son of God? Have you come here to torment us before the time?"

A long way off from them, a large herd of pigs was feeding. "If you drive us out," the demons begged him, "send us into the herd of pigs."

Matthew 8:28–31

I used to not pay too much attention to the names of cities and regions in the Bible. I didn't know how much difference it made if Jesus was heading to Capernaum, Jerusalem, or the Gadarenes. But what a difference it makes if I'm traveling to Little Rock or Honolulu or the Amazon. And so it is with the significant differences between biblical locations.

The Gadarenes was a mostly Gentile region in the Decapolis, and this would have really jumped out to the ancient Jewish reader. It was located across the Sea of Galilee on the eastern shore so you had to make a point of going there. We can safely say it was not the obvious place for Jesus to take His disciples, and yet we should be getting more and more comfortable with Jesus's pattern of leading His disciples where they often least expected to go.

Culture also plays an important role in the story. Pigs were unclean to the Jews; so were tombs, dead people, and demons. Pretty much this whole scene epitomized everything that was "out" for the Jew. In modern terms, Jesus had taken His youth group to South Beach for spring break. Not to indulge in the party scene of course but to once again show His authority over any manner of darkness. He has already displayed His power over sickness (vv. 1–17), nature (vv. 23–25), and will now show His power over evil (vv. 28–34). Matthew reminds us that nothing is out from under His rule.

When Jesus and His disciples get out of the boat, they're met by two demon-possessed men. It's worth my saying I have avoided people for far less. I have skirted clear around people who might require more of me than I'm up for giving. Yet here Jesus marches straight into the path of two men whose oppressing demons were so violent no one dared even pass their way. The demons recognized Jesus as the Son of God and feared He had come to judge them earlier than expected. So they asked to be sent into a nearby herd of pigs (numbering two thousand, per Mark 5:13). We will see tomorrow that Jesus need only say "Go," and the demons obeyed.

The appointed time of the final judgment was still to come, but the demons failed to understand that God's kingdom was breaking through in the person of Jesus, in that very moment. Even today we live in this middle ground where we expectantly wait for God's final conquering of evil while having access to His mighty power over darkness now. It's what scholars call the period of "already but not yet."

I feel this, don't you? We long for all evil to be vanquished, and at the same time we are not without the conquering forces of His peace, love, joy, truth, wisdom, and power that raised Jesus from the dead. We have this access now.

I do wonder how the wide-eyed disciples fared when they rolled onto the shore of the Gadarenes and were met with raving evil. But sometimes it takes walking through the dark with Jesus to experience firsthand His power over it. Certainly the disciples much preferred strolling with Him along the familiar cobblestones of Capernaum, or sailing on the glassy waters of Galilee in His presence (when Satan wasn't stirring up squalls), to the demon and swine-haunted Gadarenes.

But we forget that people and circumstances that appeal to us are often different from what draws Jesus. Where all we can see are unclean and scary things, He sees a suffering person languishing under oppression whom He has come to rescue. Where we see obstacles he sees opportunity.

The challenge for the disciples to follow Jesus across the lake to a group of people unlike them is the same challenge we face today. How often we avoid those who most need our love and compassion because they seem to be the least like us. But since the church is the community through whom Jesus does His rescuing, we must be willing to go to those inconvenient places, reach those in the grip of the tomb, sacrifice temporal comforts for souls that are eternal.

You never know what miracles you might be part of. Luke's Gospel tells us that one of these men became one of Jesus's disciples and the first Gentile missionary to the Gentiles (Luke 8:38–39). I want to be part of *these* transformations, don't you? Dear Christ follower, let's commit to going where Jesus calls us, to reaching out to whom He leads us.

Who is Jesus asking you to cross the lake for? He promises to go with you.

DAY 72

WELLNESS ON JESUS'S TERMS

"Go!" he told them. So when they had come out, they entered the pigs, and the whole herd rushed down the steep bank into the sea and perished in the water. Then the men who tended them fled. They went into the city and reported everything, especially what had happened to those who were demon-possessed. At that, the whole town went out to meet Jesus. When they saw him, they begged him to leave their region.

Matthew 8:32–34

Healing can be surprisingly disruptive. Counselors know this, which is why they prepare you for how testy your friends and family might get when you start changing any kind of behavioral habits for the better. When one person starts to get healthy in any realm, it can really mess with the delicate equilibrium of one of our favorite human practices: good old-fashioned codependency. Apparently, it's been around for a while.

When Jesus commanded the demons into the swine, thereby saving the lives of two men, it set off a chain reaction that shook the region. Not everyone was happy about a couple of demon-possessed men getting free. First, this meant approximately two thousand swine drowned, a major blow to the local economy (remember, the Decapolis area was largely Gentile, a people who had no problem with pigs). This then drove the men who were tending the herd into the city, surely fleeing in panic and disbelief, relaying everything they saw. The whole town and countryside got wind of the disruption, and off they marched to Jesus, bristly and buzzing as we do when we're working off foggy details and up in arms over unfamiliar circumstances. The town begged Him to leave their region, and we know from Luke's Gospel they made this request because "they were overcome with fear" (8:37 NIV).

I hope fear is not causing you to push Jesus away.

They were afraid of their norms being upset. They were comfortable avoiding plagued and tormented people so long as they could carry on with their preferred lifestyles. What seemed like a cause for celebration—Jesus delivering two men, settling them back into their right minds—turned into a plea for Him to leave the area immediately. This is the problem with Jesus's kingdom: He doesn't take over only the parts we want Him to. When He comes in, He comes for every part of us. And when He shines His light in our lives, it reflects on others, and not everyone is happy about this. Sometimes we're not even happy about it.

One wise thinker sums this up beautifully: "If we have to choose between a life we know, even a life possessed by demons and ruled by death, and a life of uncertainty to which Jesus calls us, a life that may well expose us to dangers in Jesus's name, we too may ask Jesus to leave our neighborhood."[106]

We can't very well look smugly upon the people of the Gadarenes who pushed Jesus away because have we not been guilty of the same? Do we not see ourselves reflected in this story?

It's an easy thing to forge well-worn paths that go wide around those who need Jesus simply because of the darkness we might encounter if we meet them where they are. But aren't these the ones Jesus has called us to? And don't we sometimes, perhaps without realizing it, set the value of our earthly treasures (our herd of swine) above human souls (the two men)? To the people of the Decapolis, these newly freed men weren't worth the price of their livestock.

I imagine this frightful town wouldn't have minded so much if Jesus had kept His exorcism confined to the tombs, as long as it didn't affect their lives in any way. But that is to ask Jesus to bring His healing to us on our terms. We ask for a little of His salve here, some supernatural balm there, but only where we want it because we're happy with our other areas of dysfunction. But if we want to experience Jesus's healing on His terms, we must greet Him on the shore of our lives and say, "Lord Jesus, come have Your way!"

Jesus won't be confined because light spreads and the news of healing travels, and sometimes new life brings uncomfortable growing pains for ourselves and those around us. But we dare not ask Jesus to leave us alone. Whatever familiar comforts or patterns we're hanging onto can't compare to the light and healing He desires to bring. So we pray, *Stay, Lord Jesus, stay, no matter what.*

DAY 73

OUR COLLECTIVE FAITH

So he got into a boat, crossed over, and came to his own town. Just then some men brought to him a paralytic lying on a stretcher. Seeing their faith, Jesus told the paralytic, "Have courage, son, your sins are forgiven."

Matthew 9:1–2

The fear of being left alone is a chief fear of many. It's one of my own and the reason I'm drawn to this story of kinship, of one man being carried to Jesus by four friends. We're not supposed to journey alone. As we saw in Jesus's Sermon and now throughout His personal encounters, following Him is a communal endeavor. When Jesus calls us, He calls us into a family where we carry one another, help one another, and—what we sometimes overlook—have *faith* for one another.

We know from Mark's and Luke's Gospels that the paralyzed man and his friends at first tried to enter the house where Jesus was teaching, but they couldn't because of the crowds. Entering through the door was impossible. None of the Gospel accounts tell us whose idea it was to climb up the side of the house, dig a hole in the roof, and let down their friend in the middle of the room to get him to Jesus. Perhaps everyone had the same idea at once, but I doubt it. There's always that one person crazy enough to believe that whatever it takes to get someone to Jesus is worth the effort, even if it means a bit of demolition and acrobatics. This usually helps the rest of us follow along, hoisting our corner of the mat because faith inspires faith.

That Jesus forgave the paralyzed man's sins after having seen *their* faith is something I hope we will never get over. Despite the theological questions this tends to raise (such as, Was the paralytic's faith part of the "their" or did Jesus forgive this man's sins based solely on the faith of others?), at the very least we learn one thing: *our faith affects other people.*

This is at once a privilege and a responsibility. Can Jesus see your faith in Him for others? Is it a visible faith that carries mats, scales walls, intercedes in prayer, shares the gospel, generously gives, teaches vacation Bible school, loves one's neighbor? Sometimes we think of our faith as a personal, invisible, immaterial entity, but look at the faith of the friends in this story! When they lowered their loved one through the thatched roof, each clutching his end of the rope, teeth clenched and biceps quivering, Jesus looked up and thought, *Now, that's a faith I can see!*

When it comes to the people in your life who don't know Jesus, what faces come to mind that you can intercede for? What person or marriage or family needs to be reminded of our Savior's love? Who needs to be picked up and taken to church because he or she can no longer drive? Who can drive just fine but requires a little prodding? What friend could use some of your resources? Who might be secretly wishing you'd get over your fear of being rejected and tell them straight up about the hope you have in Christ?

Who needs to be carried to Jesus?

The image of four friends carrying another friend to the Savior is the essence of who we must be for one another in the church. Sometimes we get lazy, and we just hope the "weaker" brothers and sisters will get their act together and work it out for themselves. But this is not collective faith that Jesus can *see.*

Jesus's half brother James says that if our faith is genuine it will express itself in godly actions (James 2:14–26). Perhaps you know someone who can't get to Jesus without your help. What corner of the mat is yours to take up? What wall might you climb or roof might you open up for someone? Maybe you're the one who's supposed to lead with the crazy, improbable idea first so others will follow. This may seem like heroics, but it's better than that. It's about faith that goes beyond just yourself.

DAY 74

THE GREATEST MIRACLE OF ALL

Seeing their faith, Jesus told the paralytic, "Have courage, son, your sins are forgiven."

Matthew 9:2

The once-paralyzed man and his friends had traveled to Jesus, most certainly their last-ditch effort, hoping and believing that if they could just get to Him, He would make their friend walk. Imagine the disappointment, the hope deferred, when they rounded the corner, exhausted from carrying their friend, and their friend weary from being carried, only to see a million other people in their way. Ah, but, "wait a minute," someone says, "all is not lost! We can go through the roof!" It's an absurd, implausible idea. But anything is worth a try.

They manage to hoist their friend to the top of the house, awkwardly I imagine because this isn't the sort of thing you can practice. The friends dig through the thatched roof (hoping the owners have insurance) and slowly lower their friend into the middle of a packed house where Jesus is teaching. This grand interruption had to be humiliating for the paralyzed man, and what about the fear of being dropped or just plain disappointed? What if he'd come here for nothing? But Jesus moves toward him with kindness and compassion. Perhaps surprisingly, he hears Jesus call him by the endearing term "son." At the sound of Jesus's warm words "take courage," his fear and humiliation dissolve.

It's about to happen, he thinks to himself. *Jesus is going to heal me. I'm gonna walk out of here!*

And then the strangest thing happens. Instead of saying, "Rise," or "Get up," or "Start dancing," Jesus says, "Your sins are forgiven."

What?

This is so . . . *disappointing*—like the person on the game show hoping for the car but coming home with the refrigerator. Forgiveness of sins isn't terrible, but it's not the same as walking, we think. It's not what this man had come for.

Jesus hadn't forgotten why he and his friends had come. He wasn't aloof to this man's immobile legs or stiff joints, his life lived at the mercy of others. Jesus knew his frame and He knows yours too. He is not indifferent to what pains you, what sometimes keeps you on the mat. God promises to draw near to the brokenhearted, to bind up wounds and bottle tears (Ps. 147:3; 56:8).

Oh, beloved, He sees you. But what is so wonderful and trustworthy about Jesus is that He will never offer you less than what He knows you need.

For the paralyzed man, working legs was incredible, but forgiveness of sins was better. To be forgiven is the miracle of a running and leaping soul, cut loose from paralyzing shame and guilt. Jesus was doing for this man what He had come to do for all of us—forgive our sin so we can live free of its debilitating curse. The forgiven sinner knows what this is like!

It really is true that unforgiven sin is a far worse malady to live with than a body that doesn't work all that well. Eventually our physical bodies will be resurrected without a trace of hardship or dysfunction. But sin, when not forgiven as a result of Jesus's death on the cross, has the power to *eternally* wreak havoc on us both physically and spiritually. When we receive Jesus's forgiveness, we're not just getting a cruel weight off our backs; we are at once reconciled to God now and forever. To be forgiven is to be made well, to be given new limbs fit to run on the paths of righteousness.

It is good to seek Jesus for physical and emotional and psychological healing. But if you have yet to seek His forgiveness for your sin, then you are only seeking temporary salves for temporary ailments. Take courage today. Ask Him for forgiveness, to wash you of your sin, to lift shame and remove guilt, and you will experience the greatest miracle of all.

Forgiveness of sins may not always be our greatest want, but it has ever been our greatest need.

DAY 75

AUTHORITY TO FORGIVE SINS

At this, some of the scribes said to themselves, "He's blaspheming!"

Perceiving their thoughts, Jesus said, "Why are you thinking evil things in your hearts? For which is easier: to say, 'Your sins are forgiven,' or to say, 'Get up and walk'? But so that you may know that the Son of Man has authority on earth to forgive sins"—then he told the paralytic, "Get up, take your stretcher, and go home." So he got up and went home. When the crowds saw this, they were awestruck and gave glory to God, who had given such authority to men.

Matthew 9:3–8

The miracle of forgiveness is not always as immediately visible as the miracles of physical healing, but it is no less real. When I moved to Nashville over twenty years ago, I swiftly met some of my closest, lifelong friends. It turns out that two decades of friendship is a good amount of time to watch the miracle of Christ's forgiveness play out in one another's life. Being forgiven by Jesus is not merely a "moment of salvation"; it's a new life we grow into—a life where righteousness is possible and sin no longer has the last word in our actions and decisions. Over time, as we participate with the Holy Spirit's work in our lives, we miraculously change. This process, as you probably already know, is called *sanctification*, and if you've seen it happen in the life of another person (or in your own life), you know what a miracle it is.

But the religious leaders who were present the day Jesus forgave the paralytic's sins weren't about to wait around to see the slowly evolving effects of a possible miracle. Their hearts were hard, and they were only interested in discovering evidence that affirmed their already-held beliefs about Jesus. They now had reason to conclude that Jesus was a blasphemer since only God can forgive sins.

Jesus knew the evil thoughts they were thinking so He asked them a question: Is it easier to tell someone that their sins are forgiven, or to tell a paralyzed man to get up and walk? No matter which one is easier to *do*, it's easier to *say* that someone's sins are forgiven simply because this can't be readily verified.[107] What theological drama the paralyzed man had been lowered into! He just wanted to be able to walk. He had come for healing, and the whole thing had turned into a religious uproar.

These kinds of uproars happen because Jesus divides humanity in two—either you believe Him to be the Son of God, or you do not. Either He has authority to forgive sins, or He does not. And what you believe about Him determines absolutely everything you believe about yourself, others, God, and the world. This was the skirmish the paralytic and his friends had descended into, and it's a conversation many are having today: Is Jesus really God?

After Jesus forgave the man's sins, Jesus healed him, and out he walked with his mat in hand. This everyone could see. Meaning, what they could not see—forgiveness of sins—had also taken place. The crowds would have been able to witness the effects of this forgiveness over time, had they cared to watch. A few glorified God for giving authority to forgive sins to "men." But even they seemed to miss the point. Jesus was not one of many men who had authority to do this; He was the only one who could do it, the Son of Man (a Messianic title found in Dan. 7:13–14).

The authority that Jesus has on earth to forgive sins is still to this day the most radical miracle of all. We sometimes miss this because it's not always the most visible, at least not at first. But forgiveness of sins is salvation, and salvation means the Holy Spirit is living inside you, and the Holy Spirit living inside you is power to live the "greater righteousness" of Christ. This righteousness becomes more and more visible to others, so much so that people might just think you are a miracle and give glory to God.

Jesus, I give You glory today as the only one with the power to forgive my sin. I receive Your forgiveness and expectantly look for the day-to-day transformation You will bring about in my life. Help me walk in the way of righteousness You have prepared for me as your child.

DAY 76

GET UP AND FOLLOW

As Jesus went on from there, he saw a man named Matthew sitting at the tax office, and he said to him, "Follow me," and he got up and followed him.

While he was reclining at the table in the house, many tax collectors and sinners came to eat with Jesus and his disciples. When the Pharisees saw this, they asked his disciples, "Why does your teacher eat with tax collectors and sinners?"

Matthew 9:9–11

Tax collectors in Scripture get special billing. Often delineated from regular sinners, the tax collectors were a special breed of bad. Their own people considered them traitors because they worked for oppressive Rome. They were known for being crooked in their dealings, charging their fellow citizens more than what was required so they could pocket the rest.[108] The Jewish sentiment toward tax collectors might be similar to how we feel about the wealthy who live above the law or CEOs who nickel-and-dime their employees while flitting about on private jets. They're just not our favorites. And we have no plans to invite them to Bible study.

Jesus, however, walks by Matthew the tax collector's booth, perhaps located on the edge of town on the Sea of Galilee, and speaks the two words that have been changing lives for two millennia: "Follow Me." Jesus is putting forth an unmistakable invitation to discipleship. This will end up really frying the Pharisees, and if we're honest, it sometimes fries us. No matter how much we think we believe in God's grace for sinners, it seems we carry about this tape measure in our pockets, ready to whip out at a moment's notice to determine if someone's sin has indeed run past what's acceptable for discipleship to Jesus. In other words, we believe in grace but only within reason.

We don't know what Matthew already knew about Jesus, or whether he was miserable in his job or laden with shame, but something about Jesus's call must have made Matthew think, *Someone good wants me.*

There is so much more I want to know about this story, but perhaps all we need to know is that Jesus made His way to a sinner's sinner and asked him to leave his dead-end toll booth for a life of goodness and wholeness that would exceed that of the religious leaders. Moreover, Jesus shortly thereafter pulls up a chair at a table in Matthew's home and enjoys a remarkable feast with him and his friends. Invitations had apparently been addressed to several other "sinners" and "tax collectors."

That Jesus and His disciples were fraternizing with irreligious outsiders was troubling to the Pharisees, and it can be troubling to us. We'll reflect tomorrow on what they didn't understand about this scene, what we might not understand, but today I wonder if we might do well to pull up our own chair to Matthew's table and think about grace for a moment.

We often mistake grace as a blanket affirmation of whoever we are and however we want to live. But Jesus was not rubber-stamping everyone's choice sins at Matthew's banquet that evening. This was not a party where sinners felt comfortable because Jesus affirmed their sin; rather it was a table around which sinners felt loved because He had come to *forgive* their sin. It does not seem coincidental that Jesus would invite Mathew, a tax collector, to follow Him and that He would dine with sinners fresh on the heels of having revealed Himself as the One with authority to forgive sins. What better way for Jesus to put forgiveness to good use than to go looking for people who wanted a new start in life, who wanted to believe change was possible?

Do you feel you're too far gone, or that there's no way out of some besetting sin that is your version of the tax booth, or that you've tried to change and failed too many times to hope again? If Jesus called Matthew to leave his booth for an unexpected role as one of His twelve disciples, is He not also calling you? You may think you don't deserve it, but being one of Jesus's disciples is always undeserved whether He calls you from the tax booth or the temple.

If today you hear Jesus say, "Follow Me," instead of rehearsing the many reasons you don't deserve the chance, do what Matthew did straightaway: get up and follow Him.

DAY 77

ARE YOU SICK OR WELL?

When the Pharisees saw this, they asked his disciples, "Why does your teacher eat with tax collectors and sinners?"

Now when he heard this, he said, "It is not those who are well who need a doctor, but those who are sick. Go and learn what this means: I desire mercy and not sacrifice. For I didn't come to call the righteous, but sinners."

Matthew 9:11–13

I sympathize with the Pharisees in this story. Not because of their self-righteousness, judgmentalism, or the evil in their hearts that Jesus speaks of, rather their trying to understand the seemingly new set of rules. They had great respect for Moses's law, and they saw how badly the irreligious were messing things up for Israel. If Israel was to get on God's good side again, they were going to have to start keeping the rules. The tax collectors and sinners were the chief lawbreakers, and in the eyes of the Pharisees, they were the most obstinate roadblocks to Israel's getting back on track.

So I sympathize with how confusing it must have been for the Pharisees, all huddled together in their holy robes, one eye pouring over their scrolls, the other eye squinting disapprovingly through the window at Jesus dining with sinners. Which is it: Moses's law or a free-for-all?

It turns out, it's neither, but not in a perfectly cut-and-dried sort of way. In some ways, the path to righteousness *is* through Moses's law, but only as fulfilled in the person of Jesus. And entering God's kingdom is certainly not a free-for-all, but it is *available to all*, once again to those who come through Jesus. This is where it got confusing for the Pharisees and where it can get confusing for us. Why *was* Jesus eating with the reprobates, the anything-goes type of people, when holiness was such a big deal to Him? Such a big deal to God? Because, according to one of my favorite thinkers, "It seems that holiness begins with the recognition that we are not well."[109] This was what the religious leaders refused to admit about themselves. And it is still to this day one of the greatest barriers to faith in Jesus—recognizing that we are not well and therefore need a Savior.

The Pharisees in many respects had the right definition of holiness, but they had the wrong idea that they could achieve it themselves as well people, when in fact they were as sick as the tax collectors—they just hadn't gotten the results of their blood work back. They had equally overlooked major parts of God's law, like loving one's neighbor, honoring one's parents, speaking truth. Perhaps their biggest miss? Showing mercy.

In response to the Pharisees' question about why Jesus was eating with sinners, Jesus dipped back into the book of Hosea and reminded them of what God had spoken: "I desire mercy and not sacrifice," meaning He desires mercy *more* than sacrifice.[110] Hosea hadn't done away with the sacrificial system; rather he was revealing that love triumphed over religious ritual.[111] The Pharisees had somehow disregarded this, which is why they couldn't bear to accept Jesus's companionship with sinners around a lavish table of feasting. They refused to see that the temporal, recurring sacrifices of the sacrificial system would one day be fully satisfied through the once-and-for-all sacrifice of Christ, a sacrifice of mercy.

Back to my sympathizing with the Pharisees. If they had earnestly been seeking God, they would have recognized His merciful heart being expressed through the actions of Jesus. They would have been in touch with their own sickness, their own need of a Savior who wants to make well the unholy. The rules hadn't really changed as much as the Pharisees' heart had been exposed: they thought spiritual wellness could be achieved through law-keeping instead of wholly through Jesus. Matthew and his guest list of sinners on the other hand were certain it could only be obtained by mercy, the mercy of Jesus who had come to make the sick righteous.

Dearest Jesus, do not let us be sick people masquerading as well. We want be holy because You have made us so by Your mercy. We know we need You and are ever grateful You came to seek and to save the lost.

DAY 78

GETTING THROUGH THE WINDOW

Then John's disciples came to him, saying, "Why do we and the Pharisees fast often, but your disciples do not fast?"

Jesus said to them, "Can the wedding guests be sad while the groom is with them? The time will come when the groom will be taken away from them, and then they will fast."

Matthew 9:14–15

This terribly distracting bee is trying to escape my porch through a closed window, and he is relentless with his frenzied buzzing, battering his body against the glass over and over. I can feel his frustration, and I would like to help him except I actually don't care enough to leave my chair. His is a maddening situation because everything looks normal through the glass—the sky, the waving tree branches, the other flying creatures zipping by, and therein lies the problem: the windowpane that stands between him and the great outdoors does not inhibit what he can see but where he can *go*. He is imprisoned, he doesn't understand why, and he is mad about it.

The religious leaders of Jesus's day keep bumping up against a similar pane of glass. They have eyes to see the law, they can read the commandments on the parchment, but they can't seem to get free. This time it is neither the Pharisees nor the scribes but John the Baptist's followers who are trying to make sense of things. Why aren't Jesus and His disciples fasting, they want to know, like they themselves and the Pharisees often fast? And how come Jesus and His followers are carrying on in a joyous celebration, eating and drinking (Luke 5:33)? Wasn't fasting a regular practice of the Scriptures?

You can hear the buzzing, the ruckus against the glass.

Jesus gently opens the window for them, but it's not one everyone wants to go through. He explains that a wedding is no time for sadness; rather it's a time for feasting and celebration. Jesus is the bridegroom, a Messianic term, and His disciples are as His closest wedding guests. How could anyone mourn or fast at such a joyous time? Of course, if you were one of the ones who saw Jesus as merely another religious figure, another leader of a new sect of Judaism, well then best keep fasting. Business as usual is what the religious leaders seemed most comfortable with, even if it meant sackcloth. But if Jesus was the Son of God in their midst, shouldn't they be feasting?

Jesus said there would soon be real cause for fasting and mourning, the day He would be "taken" from His followers, a violent term depicting His crucifixion in veiled terms. But until that day, joy and feasting were in order for those in His presence. While theirs was a celebration of His earthly, physical presence that had ushered in the kingdom, we too have cause for such joy today. After Jesus was taken from the disciples, He rose from the dead and gave us the companionship of His Spirit.

Jesus is *with* you right now, even if not in the flesh.

This world is an awfully broken place, and while we wait for Christ to return and fully redeem all things, there's a place for fasting and mourning and lament. But in our present circumstances there's also reason for laughter and feasting, singing and dancing, joy and celebration. We believe that Jesus is the Messiah, the Son of God, the forgiver of sins, the one with authority over darkness and disease, the bridegroom who is one day coming back for His bride. We don't have to earn our way into this wedding feast; we simply must follow Jesus into it.

The bee is still knocking around on my porch. What is even worse from my vantage point is that just a few inches away is an open window of escape he for some reason is not taking. For the bee's part I assume this is ignorance; for the Pharisees, scribes, and John's disciples it feels more like obstinance. For us, I pray we will not resist the grace found in Jesus. We need not batter ourselves against the glass. We not only have eyes to see; we've been set free! May we join Him at the table of celebration because He has made a way for us to.

DAY 79

PATCHES AND WINESKINS

"No one patches an old garment with unshrunk cloth, because the patch pulls away from the garment and makes the tear worse. And no one puts new wine into old wineskins. Otherwise, the skins burst, the wine spills out, and the skins are ruined. No, they put new wine into fresh wineskins, and both are preserved."

Matthew 9:16–17

My sister Katie loves house design, and when she visits, we often rearrange my furniture, which means hauling large pieces like armoires, sideboards, and chests from room to room to see where each one best "speaks." Sometimes we decide that I simply need something new. On one occasion we hopped all over Nashville collecting everything from a new light fixture to some small pictures to a dining room table. Everything I brought home either leaned old or French. I stood back and took in the classic candelabra whimsically hanging over the antique table. "You know," I said dumbfounded, "I'm not as modern as I thought." Katie looked at me as if she could see all self-awareness had drained from my body. "Kelly," she asserted, "You don't have a modern bone in your body."

It is true I like old and classic, and if I were sitting with Jesus listening to His descriptions about old patches of cloth and old wineskins, I might've been inclined to clutch those ancient forms of Judaism, to see them preserved. What is it about the "old way of doing things" that often feels safer than the new, like pulling a well-worn blanket to your face, smelling its familiar scent, even if it can no longer keep you all that warm? The freshness of Jesus's kingdom, the soft hearts and new spirits of which Jeremiah and Ezekiel had spoken, had arrived. If the new patch of His kingdom of grace were stitched onto the old fabric of fading sacrificial systems and temple rituals, they would tear apart from each other almost immediately. Likewise, how could the fermenting, bubbling wine of the gospel that would reach to all the nations possibly be contained in the old wineskins of the ancient Jewish system without bursting open?

John's disciples were concerned that Jesus's disciples had forsaken the "old way of doing things," in this case by not fasting. But people fasted when they were overwhelmed, desperate for God's help in dire situations. This is clearly not necessary when God in the flesh is in your midst, sitting next to you at dinner. But that was the problem. John's disciples didn't see Jesus that way. They and the religious leaders didn't understand how He fit into their ancient forms of doing things, and the truth is, He didn't fully. No, the law could not contain Jesus, but in Jesus the law would be contained (Matt. 5:17). The old ways of Judaism could only find their intended fulfillment in Him.

Lest we be too hard on John's disciples, we still allow our religious ways of doing things to compete with our new life in Jesus. We may not be up in arms about who's not fasting, but we can get pretty worked up about all sorts of things that have little to do with what Jesus has already taught us is important to Him: loving our neighbors and even our enemies, treasuring our marriages, not being quick to anger, going the extra mile, living generously, not judging, not worrying, being salt and light. Some of the religious practices we've grown comfortable with can stand in the way of the fresh work Jesus is doing in our lives.

Are you trying to sew the new life of Jesus onto a tired religious cloth? Are you wishing to pour the fresh wine of His kingdom into brittle skins of rule-keeping? Like fasting, our favorite traditions are meaningful, our dearly held biblical commandments are solidly good, but only so far as they find their ultimate aim in Jesus.

Dearest Jesus, show me what inherited traditions or cherished preferences aren't serving Your new kingdom purposes in my life. I don't want anything to stand in the way of loving You more deeply and serving You more fully. I confess that old affinities cannot compare to Your new wine.

DAY 80

JESUS AND OUR TIMETABLES

As he was telling them these things, suddenly one of the leaders came and knelt down before him, saying, "My daughter just died, but come and lay your hand on her, and she will live." So Jesus and his disciples got up and followed him.

Just then, a woman who had suffered from bleeding for twelve years approached from behind and touched the end of his robe, for she said to herself, "If I can just touch his robe, I'll be made well."

Jesus turned and saw her. "Have courage, daughter," he said. "Your faith has saved you." And the woman was made well from that moment.

Matthew 9:18–22

In verses 18–26, Matthew rolls two miracles for us into one: the healing of a grown woman and the resurrection of a young girl. Had the two miracles happened days apart, neither would have lost its meaning or magnificence, but we would have missed an important lesson: God is not limited by our timetables. You see, the story of these two urgent situations (a dying girl and a bleeding woman) remind us of how hemmed in we are by this thing we call *time*. And that Jesus is not beholden to it.

Jairus's situation is dire. His precious daughter has just died (Luke's Gospel says "dying"), and He needs Jesus to get to her at the speed of an ambulance. Jesus and His disciples immediately follow Jairus because nothing is more urgent, nothing is more critical than reaching this synagogue leader's daughter. From our perspective it's a full-on race against the clock. Anything less than a frenzied, panicked sprint toward Jairus's home feels insufficient. We expect to see Jesus and His disciples knocking people over and running into fruit stands to get there, sending clusters of grapes and pomegranates flying.

And yet not one piece of flying fruit appears. Instead, the urgency of the moment is interrupted by a woman who has been bleeding for twelve years, the number of years Jairus's daughter had been alive. She determined that if she could but touch the hem of Jesus's robe she would be healed. And she was right. Luke tells us that the moment she brushed his garment, her bleeding stopped instantly (Luke 8:44). From an efficiency standpoint, this is wonderful news because the woman now has a clean bill of health and Jesus can keep going. In fact, it appears she had caught Him midstride so, praise God, she is healed and not a second has been lost. *Everyone, as you were.*

But this is not what happens. Jesus does the unthinkable. He stops and asks this woman a question that, in light of Jairus's languishing daughter, seems peculiarly unnecessary and trivial. "Who touched me?" He asks (Luke 8:45). Pretty much everyone had touched Him. After all, He had been making his way through the crowds. But here alongside Jesus's disciples we too must pause. Even if you know how this story ends, pretend you don't. Feel your blood pressure rise on behalf of Jairus as you witness Jesus operate outside of His urgent timetable by stopping for a woman He's already cured. It's beyond comprehension.

This story reminds me of how one-dimensional and finite we are as humans. It reminds me how anxious I can get inside time's pressure cooker. Isn't it astounding that Jesus could fully handle Jairus, his daughter, and a bleeding woman all at the same time? That He could somehow be there for each of them, even if it seems the twelve-year-old had been put on hold. She had not. Jesus was about to do something astonishing in her that would only prove more so the longer He spoke with the woman now healed of her bleeding.

We will reflect more tomorrow on this woman's healing, and soon we will follow Jesus to the bedside of this little girl. But for now, we must remember that Jesus is not bound by time. Somehow He stands outside of it though He works within it.

What is pressing to you? What urgent matters are you disappointed that Jesus only seems to be strolling toward, maybe having even stopped altogether, when you feel He should be sprinting? Take heart today. His power is not limited by your schedule or agenda. He is sovereign over all things. His timing is spot-on. And He's working even when you don't see Him. When it seems like all is lost, remember what happens next: a resurrection.

DAY 81

TAKING AWAY OUR SHAME

Just then, a woman who had suffered from bleeding for twelve years approached from behind and touched the end of his robe, for she said to herself, "If I can just touch his robe, I'll be made well."

Jesus turned and saw her. "Have courage, daughter," he said. "Your faith has saved you." And the woman was made well from that moment.

Matthew 9:20–22

Shame is a terrible thing. As many have noted over the years: guilt says *what I did was bad*, while shame says *I am bad*. This is why shame is so awful. It doesn't just lay on top of us; it seeps in. Like when my niece Lily dropped an Andes mint onto my light wool rug and then accidentally stepped on it, grinding it into the fibers with her cute tiny sandal. Everyone in the room knew the chocolate was never fully coming out. It's part of the wool now. Shame seems to get in us like that.

Jesus knew this, which is why I believe He stopped for the bleeding woman. We know from Luke's version of the story that her hemorrhaging ceased the moment she touched the hem of His robe. This tells us there was no need for Jesus to have stopped, especially since He was unusually busy with an emergency situation. So we have to ask ourselves, Why did He linger with this woman? Why did He take time with her when she hadn't asked for it? She'd gotten what she'd come for—physical healing. What else was there?

So much more, Jesus knew. Twelve years of bleeding had left her ceremonially unclean, cut off from the temple, isolated from her community. This condition would have likely rendered her unable to bear children, which in turn would have left her unmarriable or divorced.[112] To be childless in first-century Judaism and to be fending for oneself as a single woman was an unbearable existence.[113] The ostracization, the loneliness, the shame. No wonder she had tried to slip in and slip out, imperceptibly swiping one end of one tassel, having as little contact with Jesus as necessary, leaving as little trace as possible.

Imagine her relief when after touching Jesus's robe her bleeding stopped. She could feel an immediate cure. She could escape unnoticed. Turning to leave, thinking she'd gotten out both healed and unscathed, she heard a terrifying question, "Who touched me?" For a moment, Peter unwittingly buys her time with his usual rebuttals and antics. "Who touched you, Jesus?" he exclaims. "Everyone is touching you! We're in a crowd!" But of course this isn't the kind of touch Jesus is referring to. He wants to know who touched Him with intent. With faith.

Once again, Luke tells us that when the woman knew she'd been discovered, she inched forward, trembling, and fell down in front of Jesus. She told Him her story while a stunned crowd looked on. At first this seems like an exercise in public shaming, but we soon realize it's an act of public restoration. She was an outcast whose highest hope was to be made physically whole, an aspiration far too low for what Jesus had in mind. He loved her too much to let her get away merely with her health. He wanted to take away her shame.

"Take courage, daughter" is a term of endearment, not the condemning words she must have been expecting. And instead of pointing to her uncleanliness, Jesus points to her belief: "Your faith has saved you." He wants her to understand that her healing wasn't based on superstition; rather her healing and salvation were based on the object of her faith, Jesus Christ Himself.

He had not called her forward to embarrass her but to restore her. To make her new, not just now in the presence of this crowd but forever in the sight of God.

Do you believe Jesus wants to give you more than what you've come to Him for? Do you know that He longs to defeat the enemy of shame in your life, the one that keeps you isolated, cut off from a true and open relationship with God and others?

That day, in the middle of a pressing emergency, Jesus spoke salvation over a woman laden with humiliation. She would become His daughter. She would leave in peace. She would inherit His kingdom. It was all worth stopping for after all.

Dearest Jesus, I praise you today that you consider me not only worth stopping for but dying for. Heal my wounds, wash me of my shame, and help me go today in peace.

DAY 82

A RESURRECTION STORY

When Jesus came to the leader's house, he saw the flute players and a crowd lamenting loudly. "Leave," he said, "because the girl is not dead but asleep." And they laughed at him. After the crowd had been put outside, he went in and took her by the hand, and the girl got up. Then news of this spread throughout that whole area.

Matthew 9:23–26

We've all been in desperate scenarios where our means and strength fail us, where what we're capable of pulling off falls woefully short. Jairus, the local synagogue leader, a representative of the Jewish establishment, was in such a position. He would have been privy to Jesus's miracles, but as a Jewish leader he would have also been aware of the controversy beginning to swirl around Him. But with his only daughter in peril, with everything on the line, he ran to Jesus even if doing so may have put him in the company of heretics. As much as we see Jairus's desperation, we see his faith.

Resurrections at that time were almost unprecedented, save a couple Old Testament stories. Yet Jairus believed that just a touch from Jesus's hand would be enough to bring his beloved daughter back from death. Often in desperate times we discover in what or whom we have placed our faith.

I once took a trip to Maui for a friend's birthday. Despite my strong claustrophobic misgivings about landing on a miniscule island floating in the middle of the Pacific Ocean, I went. My friends and I cashed in a decade's worth of hotel points to stay at the Ritz Carlton. In other words, for nine days we lived as impostors among the wealthy and well dressed. It was uncannily appropriate that during our short visit a text message went out to everyone on the island. It kindly read: BALLISTIC MISSILE THREAT INBOUND TO HAWAII. SEEK IMMEDIATE SHELTER. THIS IS NOT A DRILL.

For nearly thirty minutes we and the elite vacationers in our hotel lurched through the lobby in a daze. No one knew what direction to head or what questions to ask, whether to remain calm or wail. With one text message all of us were facing the limits of our humanity. The problem was that no amount of money or prestige could get any of us out of our predicament. Money can buy a lot of things, but it cannot buy you out of an incoming ballistic missile. (It turns out the text message was sent in error, having a great deal to do with why I am alive to write this devotional and am hard-pressed to return to Hawaii anytime soon.)

Whatever resources or respect Jairus had as a synagogue leader, when it came to needing a run-in with the unprecedented or the impossible, his only hope was in Jesus. Both Mark and Luke tell us that as Jesus made His way to Jairus's house a messenger brought him the tragic news that his daughter had died. There was nothing more to be done. But sometimes, even when nothing more can be done, Jesus says, "Don't be afraid; just believe."

When Jesus and Jairus arrived at the house, the professional mourners (an actual vocation back then) were already at work. They sneered at Jesus when He asked them to leave because He claimed the girl was not dead but merely sleeping. Jesus of course wasn't disputing her death, only that bringing her back to life was as doable for Him as waking her from a nap. Though Jesus had healed the bleeding woman deliberately in front of the crowds, He would perform this miracle in private. Only Jairus, his wife, Peter, James, and John were invited inside to watch Jesus "wake her up." By touching the girl's hand, Jesus yet again defied ritual uncleanliness by coming in contact with the dead. But as had been the case with Him all along, He would not be defiled by her death; rather she would be raised by His life. With a touch of His hand, she lived.

Jesus's power to resurrect Jairus's daughter would point to His own resurrection where death would be defeated once and for all. Oh yes, death still grieves us today, but it has lost its enduring sting. It is but "sleep" for the believer who will immediately wake up in the presence of our risen Lord.

A day is coming, dear one, when there will be no more dying twelve-year olds, no more desperate fathers, no more bleeding women, no more ballistic missiles. The God who raised Jesus from the dead will raise us too (2 Cor. 4:14). Do you believe Him?

DAY 83

THE BLIND WITH EYES TO SEE

As Jesus went on from there, two blind men followed him, calling out, "Have mercy on us, Son of David!"

When he entered the house, the blind men approached him, and Jesus said to them, "Do you believe that I can do this?"

They said to him, "Yes, Lord."

Then he touched their eyes, saying, "Let it be done for you according to your faith." And their eyes were opened. Then Jesus warned them sternly, "Be sure that no one finds out." But they went out and spread the news about him throughout that whole area.

Matthew 9:27–31

I wonder if faith has been a confusing topic for you as it has sometimes been for me. It's easy to read Scripture, especially these miracle stories, and begin to think of faith in terms of a financial transaction or investment. How much faith do we need for God to do what we want? What's the ROI? Of course, this is not how faith works functionally, nor is getting what we want what faith is about. The way I see it, we must esteem faith for its great worth and significance (without faith, it's impossible to please God), while not using it to try to control God or earn His favor. We also must be careful not to exalt our faith to the point where it becomes the focus, even in place of Christ Himself.

Each of these miracle stories helps us discover where faith "fits" in our everyday lives, despite not giving us a consistent pattern or formula.

We might even argue that the absence of a formula tells us much of what we need to know about it: "Praiseworthy faith does not doubt God's ability to act, but it does not presume to know how he will choose to act."[114] So today, as we reflect on the faith of two blind men, may Jesus also open up our eyes to see Him more clearly and, as a result, increase our faith. Not merely so we can get what we want but so we can know Him more deeply.

Sometime after Jesus healed the bleeding woman and Jairus's daughter, whom Matthew points out as two people of faith, two blind men begin following Him, calling out, "Have mercy on us!" Like everyone else in these miracle stories, they are desperate. They understand Jesus is their only hope. Interestingly, these men don't initially address Him as "Lord" or "Teacher," but "Son of David." This is only the second mention of this title in Matthew's Gospel, the first being in chapter 1, verse 1. Though we're not sure how much the men understood of Jesus's divinity, the term is significant because it refers to His messianic lineage and royal role (2 Sam 7:11b–16).[115] As numerous thinkers have pointed out, isn't it interesting that two blind men have the spiritual eyes to see Jesus as Messiah, whereas the religious leaders, who could gaze at the evening sky or spot a bird alighting on a branch, were blinded to who Jesus really was.

Once Jesus is alone inside with the two men, He asks them if they believe He can perform this miracle. This feels like an odd question, as if Jesus first needs to check their belief credentials before He will do anything for them. But it's much more likely that Jesus is drawing out their faith. Perhaps they initially expected that He would entreat God for their healing, but Jesus wanted to show them that He could do it Himself.[116] Because He *is* God. What a privilege Jesus extends to them. What revelation. When He opens their eyes, they would not only see the frame of His face, the way His eyes looked kindly toward them; they would see His God-ness. They would see what so many others with twenty-twenty vision could not. (They would also fail to obey His command that forbade them to tell anyone what had happened. Perhaps Jesus wanted to avoid people following Him solely in response to His wonder-working power instead of His call to sacrificial discipleship).

Is Jesus stretching your faith in Himself? Is He asking you to believe not only in what He can do but in who He is? Like the blind men, we often see Jesus with the greatest clarity in our darkest times. When we are most desperate, we get to know Him even beyond His being Teacher and Lord; we find Him to be Son of David, Bread of life, Immanuel, Lamb of God, Redeemer, *Friend*.

Ask Him for great faith. And then trust Him to do whatever He in His goodness chooses.

DAY 84

MATTERS OF FAITH

Just as they were going out, a demon-possessed man who was unable to speak was brought to him. When the demon had been driven out, the man who had been mute spoke, and the crowds were amazed, saying, "Nothing like this has ever been seen in Israel!"

Matthew 9:32–33

The final miracle of Matthew's third triad of miracle stories is short and to the point. Some people—we're not even told who they are—bring a demon-possessed man to Jesus. He drives out the demon and liberates the man's speech. Surprisingly, faith is not mentioned at all. Its absence is noticeable since faith has played an important role in the past few miracles surrounding Jairus, the hemorrhaging woman, and the blind men. If we're still looking for faith formulas, this last account might send us back to the drawing board.

It is true that Jesus often performed miracles in *response* to great faith, and it is also true that He sometimes worked wonders to *instill* faith when there was little or none to be found. How else do we make sense of the disciples in the boat who had just a "little" faith, or Peter's mother in-law who is not shown to exhibit any at all, or the Roman centurion whose faith was greater than anyone in Israel's? Or what about the paralytic whose healing appears to have ridden in on the coattails of his friends' faith? Matthew's ten accounts aren't meant to confuse us. We can't earnestly read all of these stories as part of a greater whole and walk away thinking our faith isn't important to Jesus.

But as we already touched on, we also can't conclude that great faith is capable of arm-wrestling God to do what we want, nor does a lack of faith exclude Him from accomplishing something supernaturally restorative and undeserved in our lives if He so pleases. Our faith matters to the heart of Christ, but we don't exhibit it to manipulate an outcome. Rather, we exercise faith to show Jesus that we trust Him with the outcome.

Perhaps you can think back to a time when God responded to the little faith you had, stretching it through a trial as if it were pizza dough, working those edges, thickening the middle sections that were nearly see through. What began as a small amount of faith, Jesus enlarged and strengthened. I'm sure you can remember other times when you were flat on your back, or just meandering through life minding your own business, not an ounce of faith to be had, and Jesus met you in extraordinary fashion. He instilled faith in you by His mighty, unexpected, undeserved work in your life. Like the oppressed and mute man, He didn't heal you because of your great faith but to show you who He is and to grow faith within you. Faith that proves more precious than the world's most valuable offerings (1 Pet. 1:7).

We can look back through Matthew's ten miracle stories and see that whether Jesus worked miracles to show compassion to people, challenge the Jewish religious traditions, or break down cultural barriers, the most central reason He acted was to show that His kingdom had arrived. The prophet Isaiah had long ago foretold that we would know the Messiah when He came because the blind would see, the lame would walk, the lepers would be cleansed, the deaf would hear, the dead would be raised, and the poor would be told the good news (Isa. 35:5; Matt. 12:5). All of these miracles testified of His arrival.

I need to be reminded of this today. I bet you do too. You may be praying for a miracle, desperate for healing to come in your own life or the life of a loved one. Maybe you've grabbed your end of the faith rope, but the other end seems only tugged by silence. Take courage: Jesus is near those who seek Him even when we don't feel Him. He knows that on some days you have a lot of faith, others a little, maybe sometimes in the dead of night, none at all. Keep turning your attention back to who He is, One so compassionate He would touch a leper, so fiercely righteous He would drive out demons, so unrushed He would heal a woman suffering from physical and emotional bleeding, so God that He would raise the dead. And if you just don't have it in you to even lift your head toward Him, ask Him to come to you.

Dear Lord, Your Word says that without faith it is impossible to please You (Heb. 11:6). I ask You to instill faith in me where it is lacking, and where my faith is strong, will You respond in extraordinary ways? And during the seasons where it is stretched thin, where it is very "little," continue to act because of Your goodness and grace. For You, Jesus, are the Author and Finisher of my faith (Heb. 12:2).

DAY 85

WE'VE NEVER SEEN ANYTHING LIKE THIS BEFORE

When the demon had been driven out, the man who had been mute spoke, and the crowds were amazed, saying, "Nothing like this has ever been seen in Israel!"

But the Pharisees said, "He drives out demons by the ruler of the demons."

Matthew 9:33–34

Isn't it interesting that two groups of people can witness the same remarkable miracle yet come away with two vastly different opinions about who Jesus is? The crowds were amazed, but the Pharisees saw Jesus as a teammate of the demons. I find this disparity of ideas around Jesus to be the case today, don't you? For most professing nonbelievers, they're okay with Him so long as He doesn't have any bearing on their personal choices or their moral lives, so long as He is not *God*. Jesus is both exciting and polarizing this way.

Once while I was running on a treadmill, my trainer said to me, "Jesus is good for you; He is *a* way to God among many." I don't know how we got to talking about this, but it was one of those moments I wanted to brush off mostly because I am not one of those annoying people who is in shape enough to run while bantering. But her statement was about Jesus's deity, His Godhead. If He is simply "a way," how can His words mean anything of significance since He claims to be "the way"

(John 14:6)? I couldn't let the comment go unaddressed. I offered the rebuttal that Jesus Himself doesn't allow us to pick what we will of His teaching, make what we will of His deity. He cannot be the One before whom every knee will bow while simultaneously being a nice option for some. I have never regretted stopping to make that distinction because if Jesus is only *a* way, He is no way at all.

And this is why the Pharisees needed to explain Jesus's miracles away. Since there was no disputing the supernatural works He had done, they had to make a case against His identity. But the crowds exclaimed, "Nothing like this has even been seen in Israel!" I can't get these words out of my head. The awe, the astoundment, the newness.

For many of us, the miracle of our salvation works itself out in our daily circumstances, and while most days are "normal," every once in a while God astounds us. A few years into my dismal experience in the music industry, the then president of my record company invited me to the Amazon. It was a check-the-box sort of trip, something I thought would be interesting and worthwhile but nothing I imagined would be life changing. No one told me about the little kids who charge across the river in wooden canoes, the pink dolphins that dazzle in the morning hours, the jungle pastors whose faith in Jesus will bring you to your knees. I was instantly captured. God had simply and unexpectedly bowled me over with His creation, His people, and Himself. Thirty trips later and He's still showing me things "I've never seen before."

I wonder when the last time was that God wowed you beyond belief. Don't we long for Jesus to do new things in our lives we haven't seen? I think of the way young children react when they spot a dandelion, an autumn leaf, a robin's egg. You'd think they'd stumbled upon the Hope Diamond the way they look at you in disbelief, their mouths agape in utter shock and delight. I want that fresh dose of wonderment.

We must remember that the ten miracles Matthew curated for us were to show Jesus's power over sickness, evil, nature, and sin. They were mostly to show that He indeed was the long-awaited Messiah for whom the Jews, and ultimately the Gentiles, were waiting.

And as long as Jesus is God, He will remain in the miracle business. So let us seek Him today for unexplainable joy, forgiveness that exceeds our natural capacity, restored marriages, divinely appointed encounters, lost souls to be found. Let us ask Him to do a *new* thing in our lives, something that will make us say, "We've never seen anything like *this* before!" And in those in-between times, may He find us faithful followers.

When was the last time Jesus astounded you? What new thing might He be doing in your life? And if the current call is to keep doing what you're doing, ask Him to show you what you've never seen before in the middle of daily obedience.

DAY 86

FULL CIRCLE

Jesus continued going around to all the towns and villages, teaching in their synagogues, preaching the good news of the kingdom, and healing every disease and every sickness.

Matthew 9:35

WE'RE NEARING THE END OF our ninety-day journey together at the same place we began. But this doesn't mean we haven't covered ground, only that what Matthew states in verse 4:23 he closes with in 9:35, delivering us full circle. You may recall from day 1 that these verses form bookends around Matthew's anthology of Jesus's teachings, miracles, and healings. What he *summarized* in these two verses, he helped us *experience* in between. And what an experience it has been. One we must not forget.

My four-year-old niece Lily has recently decided that her brother Will's baseball games are boring. She now incessantly asks me to take her to the nearby playground during the parts of the game where not much is happening, those spans of time we call innings. I find that watching children on the playground, even ones you're crazy about, is right up there with having a tooth pulled. This is why children hound you, because eventually their begging exceeds the pain of you watching them play on a merry-go-round from a nearby bench and you acquiesce.

During one of Will's baseball games, Lily had asked me at least eleven times if I would take her to the playground. So together we walked hand in hand toward the swings while my emotional well-being began to shrivel.

"Aunt Kelly, have you ever been to this playground before?"

"Yes, dear. Don't you remember a few days ago when I took you? When it was freezing and my hands were chapped and I pushed you for ten minutes on the swings, which in playground time is ten years?"

"I don't remember that," she said, pointing to a butterfly.

I explained that she was going to have to start remembering these sacrificial acts of love from her Aunt Kelly. That I needed my efforts to count. We are funny creatures this way. After the sheen of having gotten what we wanted so badly begins to wear off, we're onto the next thing, and we wonder when the last time was that a person or even God did something for us?

So I think at least part of why Matthew repeats the verse about Jesus's teaching, preaching, and healing is to say: *don't forget*. It's to say that the words Jesus teaches are words to live by—ones that will affect your family, vocation, friendships, and finances. Words that will bring peace to your soul. It's to say that the good news of His kingdom having come to us on earth is the best news to grace humanity since Adam and Eve walked in the garden of Eden. And that Jesus healed the sicknesses and diseases of those with whom He encountered says not only that His care and compassion for you is extraordinary but that He really is God.

What has Jesus done for you in the past eighty-six days? More importantly, who has He shown Himself to be to you? What of His teachings impacted you the most? And which of His encounters with desperate individuals will you be thinking about in the days and weeks to come?

But don't think our journey has come to an end. As much as today's verse is a closing statement, it is also an opening one, like a door swinging from one adventure into the next. As we will discover in our final few days together, this verse sets the groundwork for what *we* are to do. Jesus did not spend all that time teaching His disciples about heart transformation and how to live in His kingdom, all that time showing them what meeting the tangible needs of the lost and hurting and sick looks like, for the disciples to just go on their merry ways. And the same goes for us. Jesus taught, healed, and brought good news so *we* might do the same things in our world as He did in His. As we'll soon see, Jesus will expressly show us that it's our turn now. And that our devotional's end really is but the beginning.

Lord Jesus, prepare me for what you have in store for me to do.

DAY 87

OUR COMPASSIONATE SAVIOR

When he saw the crowds, he felt compassion for them, because they were distressed and dejected, like sheep without a shepherd.

Matthew 9:36

It seems as if the world has never groaned louder than it is now. Perhaps every generation feels this way, but I've had more conversations recently about how splintered we are by disagreements, how divided we are politically, how much mental and emotional unrest there is in our American neck of the world. We're all looking for a solid and safe foundation, and it seems that much of what used to be fairly stable is now shifting beneath our feet.

It is precisely this unsettledness, this hardship, this mass of humanity trying to find its way for which Jesus has strong feelings. In other words, it was the condition of the *crowds* that really got to Him. Because they were *distressed* and *dejected*, and the reason they were these things is because they had no protector, no one leading and loving them. They didn't know where they were going—they were as *sheep* without a *shepherd*. Now I don't mean to italicize too many words, but these are five really important ones that each tell a story, words we'll look at in a moment. But none of these are as important as this word: *compassion*.

In the original language, the word for "compassion" references the seat of a person's emotions. It's a monster-sized unction of love and passion for people that literally translates as "inward parts."[117] So we get this sense that Jesus's compassion for the crowds was felt at a gut level. Think of the last time your heart broke over a tragedy or injustice. When something so unbearable happened to someone you loved that the longing you felt to bind up his or her wound or meet a gaping need was a visceral ache in your soul, something you could feel in your flesh. This is the kind of compassion Matthew speaks of. And what's more, it's a word in the New Testament that is solely attached to Jesus.[118] It's an incalculable compassion distinct to Him.

Do you know that Jesus *feels* for you? Oh, yes, He saves, He helps, He rescues, but He is also filled with compassion for you. Let that truth seep into your soul's skin.

Jesus not only saw the crowds; He bled for them, specifically because they were distressed and dejected, or harassed and cast down. The first term, *distressed*, literally means "to skin, flay, or lacerate."[119] And the second one, *dejected*, means "to be thrown down."[120] We've all experienced the pain of someone slashing into our emotions, slicing into our sense of well-being with harmful words (or with something more tactile). Other times life overtakes us as waves hurling us to the ocean floor. This is the imagery of the crowds. The people of Israel hobbled under Roman oppression, many were impoverished, others were crushed by the weight of religion. But more than anything, they were lost. They were in terrible shape because they didn't know where they were going or who was leading them.

I've been thinking about this because this feels an awful lot like our own day, doesn't it? Where "the crowds," the normal masses of humanity, are anxiously wandering from sheep pen to sheep pen, hoping for a brief respite from their inner emptiness, for a jolt of pleasure or security or enlightenment. But after a short stay the grass withers, and the brooks dry up. Time to find nourishment and security someplace else.

This is the way of the distressed crowds.

But the way of Christ is to be part of a beloved flock under His tender care. It's to know where we're going even if we don't know the details of how we'll get there because we trust the One leading us. It's to lie down in green pastures and drink from running streams because we're safe and provided for under our Shepherd's care. It's to know that He will leap the fence for us and carry us home on His shoulders when we, in our rebellion or ignorance, bound off into the woods.

Oh, the compassion of Christ that calls us from being one of the crowd to one of His children. That calls us found when once we were plainly lost.

Dear reader, His compassion is eager to lead you home. Will you let Him?

DAY 88

THE HARVEST FIELD

Then he said to his disciples, "The harvest is abundant, but the workers are few. Therefore, pray to the Lord of the harvest to send out workers into his harvest."

Matthew 9:37–38

Every November, the church I grew up in held a weeklong missions conference. An assortment of our missionaries would come from far-off lands to tell us about what God was doing in the regions they served—from the jungles of Papua, New Guinea, to the fashionable city streets of Milan, to the underground church in China, and everywhere in-between. Collectively, these were some of the most formative experiences of my growing up years. I was astounded by the transcendence of the gospel: the same message that was transforming lives in my Western, middle-class world was also casting its seeds across time zones, customs, and cultures, landing onto the soil of receptive hearts and changing lives in those places too.

At these mission conferences I learned that the harvest field "out there" was booming and that God had called a certain few to live in faraway parts of the world to be laborers in His field. It's where I decided that if the Lord were to ever call me outside of the United States, I would recommend to Him Italy (and in keeping with His signature sense of humor, He of course gave me a ministry in the Amazon jungle). It's also the place my eyes were opened to the abundant harvest right in my own backyard—the one in my school, my place of work, my extended family.

But something I do not ever recall hearing was how today's missional passage sits within the teachings and stories we've been studying so far. That is, when I heard the phrase "harvest field," what mostly came to mind was a missionary term about reaching the lost. What did *not* come to mind for some reason is the unclean leper, the outsider Roman centurion, Peter's mother-in-law flat on her back, undereager and overeager disciples who were confused about what following Jesus was all about, two Gentile demoniacs and drowning swine, a paralyzed man whose friends lowered him through a roof, self-reliant religious folks, a tax collector turned disciple, a group of John's disciples with nagging questions, a bleeding woman carrying shame, a grieving father carrying faith, a dying twelve-year-old girl, two blind men, a possessed man who couldn't hear or speak, and crowds who were like wandering sheep without a shepherd.

This is the harvest field through which Jesus has just traversed, and the needs look much like our own.

So when we hear the words "harvest field" and think of missionaries in foreign lands, or even of missional work in our own backyards, we are not wrong. But *first*, I think it helps to think of all the people we just encountered, the ones Jesus healed, encouraged, and challenged. The ones for whom He had unyielding compassion. Because Jesus's harvest field is filled with all the same ailments and problems and questions and downright hostility that are awfully familiar to us. The idea of it is neither way over there someplace, nor is it remotely tidy. It seems to me that every person we've ever known, every impossible challenge, every unbearable grief is represented in Matthew's narrative.

So before we get to what Jesus is calling us to do in our own harvest field, I think we first have to determine what our harvest field is. That it is exceedingly real and in our midst. And that we're uniquely positioned to reach the people God has placed around us, many of whom need to hear the good news of the kingdom of God. Some need instruction about how to live the life Jesus says is *blessed*. Others need a healing touch or a physical need met. If the past eighty-eight days have taught us anything, it's that Jesus *taught* and *served* in the same broken world we live in.

So, what faces come to mind? What names? What needs do the people around you have?

This is your harvest field.

Lord, will You open my eyes to the harvest field in my midst? Will You give me the compassion of Your Son Jesus and make me willing and ready to be a worker in the field to which You have called me? I want to be a faithful laborer sent out into any place You'd have me serve in Your name.

DAY 89

WHEN LISTENERS BECOME LABORERS

Then he said to his disciples, "The harvest is abundant, but the workers are few. Therefore, pray to the Lord of the harvest to send out workers into his harvest."

Matthew 9:37–38

Until this point in our journey together, Jesus has been the one doing most of the work. We've listened to Him teach while the Galilean breeze swept across our skin. We've witnessed Him maneuver through the crowds, settle storm-tossed boats, rebuke the powers of darkness, and work wonders in the company of His followers. For the most part, *He* has done the heavy lifting while we have listened and watched.

But today we reach a watershed moment in the history of God's people, a turning point for Jesus's disciples, a turning point for *us*. It's the moment when Jesus tells His followers to lift their heads (John 4:35), to let their eyes run across the horizon in every direction as far as they can see and behold the fields which are ripe for harvest. It's when He asks them to pray that the Lord of the harvest would send laborers into His field, those willing to roll up their sleeves and be His workers. It's the moment when Jesus invites us to be part of His mission.

Do you see, beloved, why this isn't the end but the beginning?

It is now *our turn*.

Jesus explains to His disciples that God's workers must be "sent"—a term that literally means "thrust out."[121] In other words, we as the church need to be hurled on out there, whether overseas or in our own hometowns because the harvest is enormous. It's overwhelming. It's bursting with people ready for the love and good news and healing of Jesus. But just as laborers are needed to harvest sheeves of grain, so Christ's servants are necessary for gathering souls.

The problem is that we often tell ourselves the people around us aren't interested in the gospel. They're too intellectual, too addicted, too wealthy, too poor, too hostile, too far gone, too hard-hearted, too wounded by the church, *too lost.* If pressed, we might try to make the case that the harvest is kind of measly right now. Maybe it was riper in Jesus's day, or perhaps it's more copious in other parts of the world where the overseas missionaries are serving.

But Jesus is clear: we don't have a harvest problem. If anything, the issue is a worker shortage. We're too busy storing up treasures on earth so we just don't have time to help with the inconvenient and self-inflicted problems of the people around us. We're too committed to our comforts to invest in the lives of others. Perhaps we've been happy as mere listeners in the church, having never moved on to being a laborer in our communities. One of the problems with this type of nominal commitment is that it's unfulfilling and, frankly, boring. It's to not live the life you were called to live. It's to miss out on the investment of lives, which is the most important investment of all because it is for precious lives that Jesus sacrificed His own.

So, what does Jesus tell us to do? He tells us to pray. To pray for more workers and pray for the grace and strength to be faithful workers ourselves! As Jesus did, we must testify of the good news, teach others about the flourishing life according to God's Word, and meet those we come across with His exceeding compassion. The harvest Jesus has called us to reap isn't measured in ounces and pounds but in wounds touched, shame lifted, storms stilled, and souls saved. Only Jesus can accomplish these things, but in the strangest turn of events, what no one could have possibly seen coming, He wants to do it *with* us. With *you.*

So maybe God is calling you to live in a faraway place and proclaim His gospel to a faraway people. Maybe He is urging you toward your own family or in your local church's ministry. But one thing is for certain: if Jesus has saved you, He has called you.

What is keeping you from laboring in the harvest field? Is it fear of rejection? Prejudice? A reluctance to forgo some of your comforts? We all have different concerns, but nothing is worth missing out on the abundant life for which you were made. And when you participate with Jesus in His mission, you will reap not only lives but an unspeakable joy that only grows in His harvest field.

DAY 90

LIFE IN THE KINGDOM

"But seek first the kingdom of God and his righteousness, and all these things will be provided for you."

Matthew 6:33

The blessed life is a life lived within the will of God. And lest the idea of God's will remain a vague or fuzzy concept to us, Jesus has laid it out for us in detail: it is to thrive even in difficult times because we have an enduring kingdom accessible to us now and one day coming in full. The blessed life is to live like salt that stalls the decay of this world and as light that dispels evil and injustice. It is to recognize that true, whole-person righteousness cannot be achieved by sheer religious willpower but by the person of Jesus who has wholly fulfilled the law for us. To live blessed is to be rid of anger, to love instead of lust, to esteem marriage, to tell the truth, to refrain from retaliating, and to love our enemies. It's to no longer live fractured before God, one foot in and one foot out, but complete and whole before Him. At rest.

Blessed living means giving, fasting, and praying not for the applause of people but for the communion and reward of being present with the living God. It's to live unencumbered, light on our feet because we're not weighed down by all the things that can be stolen or grow outdated, the stuff that always leaves us disappointed and wanting more anyhow. It's to soar like nourished birds and bloom like well-tended flowers because our heavenly Father promises to look after us. And even better than a good dad, He always keeps His word. Perhaps best of all, the blessed life is the life built on the solid rock of Christ and His Word, a life that cannot be blown over or shaken, whose foundation is sure.

This is what we learned on that grassy hillside where Jesus astounded us with His teaching and instruction. Where our hearts were convicted and we were moved to repentance, where we were refreshed and comforted and moved to worship. But the blessed life won't leave us merely learning and reflecting in Jesus's presence while overlooking a placid sea. It will also require stretching our legs and putting into practice what we've learned. It will necessitate following Him through the crops of physical and emotional needs, tending those who are desperately awaiting the nourishing sustenance and healing balm of Jesus.

So we have some work to do. The good news is that it happens to be the most fulfilling work on earth. It's the sacred task of telling the good news to those who have never heard it. It's the privilege of teaching others how they too can live the blessed life, the one that comes from listening to Christ's words and doing what He says. It's to have astounding compassion for the sick, lonely, aimless, outsider, and lost—compassion that originates with Jesus and flows through our fingertips because people not only need words; they need to be touched.

The blessed life is to carry on what Jesus inaugurated with His disciples when He handed them the keys to His kingdom. Here in this passage "the mission of the church has begun. The disciples' prayer is answered, and the answer turns out to be them."[122]

The answer turns out to be us. Me and you.

And so we will sit with Jesus on the hillside, learning from Him and obeying what He tells us to do. We will follow Him down the mountain and into His field, proclaiming the good news of His death and resurrection, teaching those around us how to live according to His Word, and tangibly loving those whose lives we intersect. This is not just a good life, or even an adventurous, hopeful, and fulfilling one. It's the life Jesus calls *blessed*.

Will you choose to live it?

NOTES

1. Craig L. Blomberg, *Jesus and the Gospels: An Introduction and Survey*, 2nd ed. (Nashville: B&H Academic, 2009), 65.

2. Blomberg, *Jesus and the Gospels*, 65.

3. Jonathan T. Pennington, "The Kingdom of Heaven in the Gospel of Matthew," *The Southern Baptist Journal of Theology* 12/1 (Spring 2008), https://equip.sbts.edu/publications/journals/journal-of-theology/sbjt-121-spring-2008/the-kingdom-of-heaven-in-the-gospel-of-matthew.

4. Jonathan T. Pennington, *The Sermon on the Mount and Human Flourishing: A Theological Commentary* (Grand Rapids, MI: Baker Academic, 2017), 102.

5. Blomberg, *Jesus and the Gospels*, 448.

6. Blomberg, *Jesus and the Gospels*, 448.

7. Pennington, *The Sermon on the Mount and Human Flourishing*, 144.

8. N. T. Wright, quoted in Scot McKnight, *Sermon on the Mount*, The Story of God Bible Commentary (Grand Rapids: Zondervan, 2013), 30.

9. John Stott, *The Message of the Sermon on the Mount: Christian Counter-Culture*, rev. ed. (London, Inter-Varsity Press, 1978), 38.

10. Stott, *The Message of the Sermon on the Mount*, 40.

11. R. D. Bergen, *1, 2 Samuel*, vol. 7, The New American Commentary (Nashville: B&H, 1996), 66–67.

12. Scot McKnight, *Sermon on the Mount*.

13. Dietrich Bonhoeffer, *The Cost of Discipleship* (New York: Touchstone, 1995), 110. ProQuest Ebook Central, http://ebookcentral.proquest.com/lib/dtl/detail.action?docID=4934305.

14. Pennington, *The Sermon on the Mount and Human Flourishing*, 89.

15. McKnight, *Sermon on the Mount*, 44.

16. McKnight, *Sermon on the Mount*, 45.

17. McKnight, *Sermon on the Mount*, 47.

18. R. T. France, *The Gospel of Matthew* (Grand Rapids, MI: Eerdmans, 2007), 169.

19. Stanley Hauerwas, *Matthew* (Grand Rapids, MI: Brazos, 2006), 61.

20. Hauerwas, *Matthew*, 65.

21. Bonhoeffer, *The Cost of Discipleship.*

22. Stott, *The Message of the Sermon on the Mount*, 57.

23. Stott, *The Message of the Sermon on the Mount*, 63.

24. Stott, *The Message of the Sermon on the Mount*, 65.

25. Stott, *The Message of the Sermon on the Mount*, 60.

26. Stott, *The Message of the Sermon on the Mount*, 60.

27. McKnight, *Sermon on the Mount*, 56.

28. Stott, *The Message of the Sermon on the Mount*, 63.

29. Stott, *The Message of the Sermon on the Mount*, 57–68.

30. Stott, *The Message of the Sermon on the Mount*, 64.

31. McKnight, *Sermon on the Mount*, 58.

32. Stott, *The Message of the Sermon on the Mount*, 65.

33. McKnight, *Sermon on the Mount*, 69.

34. Bonhoeffer, *The Cost of Discipleship*, 125.

35. Bonhoeffer, *The Cost of Discipleship*, 125.

36. Stott, *The Message of the Sermon on the Mount*, 75.

37. Pennington, *The Sermon on the Mount and Human Flourishing*, 184.

38. Reuben Welch, *We Really Do Need Each Other* (New York: Impact Books, 1982).

39. France, *The Gospel of Matthew*, 203.

40. France, *The Gospel of Matthew*, 203.

41. McKnight, *Sermon on the Mount*, 82.

42. Bonhoeffer, *The Cost of Discipleship.*

43. Dallas Willard, *Renovation of the Heart: Putting on the Character of Christ* (Colorado Springs: NavPress, 2006), 82.

44. Pennington, *The Sermon on the Mount and Human Flourishing*, 191.

45. Stott, *The Message of the Sermon on the Mount*, 94.

46. Stott, *The Message of the Sermon on the Mount*, 104.

47. McKnight, *Sermon on the Mount*, 129.

48. Stott, *The Message of the Sermon on the Mount.*

49. Stott, *The Message of the Sermon on the Mount.*

50. Bonhoeffer, *The Cost of Discipleship*, 150.

51. Bonhoeffer, *The Cost of Discipleship*, 204–205.

52. Pennington, *The Sermon on the Mount and Human Flourishing*, 70.

53. Pennington, *The Sermon on the Mount and Human Flourishing*, 204.

54. Willard, *Renovation of the Heart.*

55. Martin Luther, quoted in John Stott, *The Message of the Sermon on the Mount*, 149.

56. McKnight, *Sermon on the Mount*, 175.

57. Stott, *The Message of the Sermon on the Mount*, 149.

58. Pennington, *The Sermon on the Mount and Human Flourishing*, 227.

59. McKnight, *Sermon on the Mount*, 186.

60. Pennington, *The Sermon on the Mount and Human Flourishing*, 240.

61. Pennington, *The Sermon on the Mount and Human Flourishing*, 241.

62. Pennington, *The Sermon on the Mount and Human Flourishing*, 241–42.

63. Pennington, *The Sermon on the Mount and Human Flourishing*, 239.

64. R. T. France, *Matthew: An Introduction and Commentary*, vol. 1 (Downers Grove, IL: InterVarsity Press, 1985), 143.

65. K. H. Rengstorf (1964–), μανθάνω, καταμανθάνω, μαθητής, συμμαθητής, μαθήτρια, μαθητεύω. G. Kittel, G. W. Bromiley, and G. Friedrich, eds.,

Theological Dictionary of the New Testament (electronic ed., vol. 4) (Grand Rapids, MI: Eerdmans, 1964), 414.

66. Hauerwas, *Matthew*, 82.

67. Willard, *Renovation of the Heart*, 212.

68. C. S. Lewis, *Mere Christianity* (San Francisco: HarperOne, 2015).

69. Pennington, *The Sermon on the Mount and Human Flourishing*, 256.

70. Pennington, *The Sermon on the Mount and Human Flourishing*,
71. McKnight, *Sermon on the Mount*, 238–39.

72. Pennington, *The Sermon on the Mount and Human Flourishing*,
73. Willard, *Renovation of the Heart*, 228–29.

74. N. T. Wright, *Matthew for Everyone*, Part 1 (The New Testament for Everyone) (Louisville: Westminster John Knox, 2004), 52–53. ProQuest, Ebook Central.

75. Craig L. Blomberg, *Matthew: An Exegetical and Theological Exposition of Holy Scripture* (Vol. 22, The New American Commentary), (Nashville: Holman Reference, 1992), 130.

76. Leon Morris, *The Gospel according to Matthew* (The Pillar New Testament Commentary) (Grand Rapids, MI: Eerdmans, 1992), 172.

77. Blomberg, *Matthew*, 131.

78. McKnight, *Sermon on the Mount*, 250–51.

79. Lewis, *Mere Christianity*.

80. Pennington, *The Sermon on the Mount and Human Flourishing*, 279.

81. Barbara Kingsolver, *Animal, Vegetable, Miracle* (New York: Harper Perennial, 2017), 229.

82. Pennington, *The Sermon on the Mount and Human Flourishing*, 281.

83. Donald A. Hagner in Jonathan T. Pennington, "The Kingdom of Heaven in the Gospel of Matthew," 281.

84. Dietrich Bonhoeffer, *The Cost of Discipleship*, 197.

85. France, *The Gospel of Matthew*, 299.

86. Pennington, *The Sermon on the Mount and Human Flourishing*, 282.

87. W. D. Davies, *Setting of the Sermon on the Mount* (Brown Judaic Studies) Newcastle upon Tyne, England, 1989), 435, quoted in France, The Gospel of Matthew, 299.

88. See Pennington, *The Sermon on the Mount and Human Flourishing*, 140–41; see also Blomberg, *Matthew*, 97.

89. Hauerwas, *Matthew*, 93.

90. Hauerwas, *Matthew*, 93.

91. Blomberg, *Matthew*, 139.

92. Craig S. Keener, "Matthew 8:3," *Commentary on the Gospel of Matthew*, vol. 1 (Downers Grove, IL: InterVarsity Press, 1997).

93. Christopher J. H. Wright, *The Mission of God: Unlocking the Bible's Grand Narrative* (Grand Rapids, MI: InterVarsity Press, 2006), 507, ProQuest Ebook Central, http://ebookcentral.proquest.com/lib/dtl/detail.action?docID=2033595.

94. Blomberg, *Matthew*, 143.

95. Blomberg, *Matthew*, 143.

96. Blomberg, *Matthew*, 143.

97. Leon Morris, *The Gospel according to Matthew* (The Pillar New Testament Commentary) (Grand Rapids, MI: Eerdmans, 1992), 188.

98. France, *The Gospel of Matthew*, 323.

99. Craig S. Keener, "Matthew 8:17," *Commentary on the Gospel of Matthew*, vol. 1 (Downers Grove, IL: InterVarsity Press, 1997).

100. Blomberg, *Matthew*, 147.

101. Craig S. Keener, "Matthew 8:21–22," *Commentary on the Gospel of Matthew*, vol. 1 (Downers Grove, IL: InterVarsity Press, 1997).

102. Keener, "Mathew 8:21–22," *Commentary on the Gospel of Matthew*.

103. Consider the way the Amplified Bible renders Matthew 8:21: "Another of the disciples said to Him, "Lord, let me first go and bury my father (collect my inheritance)."

104. I owe this concept to Jen Wilkins as taught in this message which can be found at http://www.tvcresources.net/resource-library/classes/worker-of-miracles.

105. Blomberg, *Matthew*, 150.

106. Hauerwas, *Matthew*, 98.

107. Blomberg, *Matthew*, 154.

108. Blomberg, *Matthew*, 156.

109. Hauerwas, *Matthew*, 101.

110. Blomberg, *Matthew*, 157.

111. Blomberg, *Matthew*, 157.

112. Craig S. Keener, "Matthew 9:20–21," *Commentary on the Gospel of Matthew*, vol. 1 (Downers Grove, IL: InterVarsity Press, 1997).

113. Keener, "Matthew 9:20–21," *Commentary on the Gospel of Matthew*.

114. Blomberg, *Matthew*, 161.

115. Blomberg, *Matthew*, 52.

116. John Chrysostom, *Homilies on St. Matthew, in Leon Morris, The Gospel according to Matthew* (The Pillar New Testament Commentary) (Grand Rapids, MI: Eerdmans, 1992).

117. H. Köster, σπλάγχνον, σπλαγχνίζομαι, εὔσπλαγχνος, πολύσπλαγχνος, ἄσπλαγχνος, G. Kittel, G. W. Bromiley, and G. Friedrich, eds., *Theological Dictionary of the New Testament* (electronic ed., vol. 7) (Grand Rapids, MI: Eerdmans, 1964), 548.

118. Morris, *The Gospel according to Matthew*, 238–39.

119. S. Zodhiates, *The Complete Word Study Dictionary: New Testament* (electronic ed.) (Chattanooga, TN: AMG Publishers, 2000).

120. Blomberg, *Matthew*, 166.

121. Blomberg *Matthew*, 167.

122. Hauerwas, *Matthew*, 104.

RESOURCES FROM

KELLY MINTER

ENCOUNTERING GOD
Cultivating Habits of Faith Through the Spiritual Disciplines
7 sessions

Unpack the biblical foundation for spiritual disciplines, including ways to practice disciplines like prayer, study, worship, rest, simplicity, generosity, celebration, and more.

ALL THINGS NEW
A Study on 2 Corinthians
8 sessions

Study the Letter of 2 Corinthians to discover how God can use you no matter your situation.

FINDING GOD FAITHFUL
A Study on the Life of Joseph
8 sessions

Trace the path of Joseph's life in the book of Genesis to observe how God's sovereignty reigns, even in our darkest moments.

WHAT LOVE IS
The Letters of 1, 2, 3 John
7 sessions

Delve into the letters of 1, 2, and 3 John, written to encourage followers of Jesus to remain faithful to the truth. Glimpse not only the heart of John but also the heart of Jesus.

NO OTHER GODS
The Unrivaled Pursuit of Christ
8 sessions

Learn to identify the functional gods you may unknowingly be serving to experience the abundant life only Jesus can give.

NEHEMIAH
A Heart That Can Break
7 sessions

Nehemiah's heart was so broken for those in need that he left the comfort of his Persian palace to help them. Are you ready to let God break your heart for a hurting, lost world and move you to be the hands and feet of Jesus?

RUTH
Loss, Love & Legacy
7 sessions

Walk through the book of Ruth and discover God's faithfulness in suffering, His immeasurable grace where we least expect it, and the way Ruth's story points toward Jesus.

A PLACE AT THE TABLE
Fresh Recipes for Meaningful Gatherings

In this beautifully photographed cookbook, Kelly Minter (along with chef Regina Pinto) shares personal stories, fresh and accessible recipes, and bonus supplemental content, inviting readers to create meaningul moments around the table.